ALL CHANGE!

THE PROJECT LEADER'S *SECRET* HANDBOOK

Eddie Obeng

MBA PhD

FINANCIAL TIMES

PITMAN PUBLISHING

For Susan

PITMAN PUBLISHING
128 Long Acre, London WC2E 9AN

A Division of Longman Group Limited

First published in Great Britain 1994

© Eddie Obeng 1994

ISBN 0 273 60762 6

Phototypeset in Linotron Times Roman, Century Schoolbook and Helvetica
by Northern Phototypesetting Co. Ltd, Bolton
Printed and bound in Great Britain
by Biddles Ltd, Guildford and King's Lynn

The Publishers' policy is to use paper manufactured from sustainable forests.

10 9 8 7 6 5 4 3 2 1

CONTENTS

PREFACE

About a year and a half ago I was teaching an executive programme on *Implementing Strategic Change through Projects*. I was in full flow when one of the participants interupted and said, 'Eddie, all this stuff is great and I feel I could use it but isn't there a book you could recommend which will remind me of your down-to-earth, common-sense approach?' 'No,' I replied, 'there isn't. What I've been teaching is about fifty per cent Eddie and fifty per cent distilled from all the books I read. Anyway,' I said, 'as a business educator that's my job. My job is to distil current thinking for you to use practically.' Another delegate piped up. 'You're wrong you know. You really should write it down.' I was surprised by the remark. I'd always assumed that the best way to transfer knowledge was through dialogue. Dialogue in the classroom. So points of view could be argued out and different opinions could be aired in the search for understanding. So I replied, 'I don't think I could stand the strain of writing a boring management textbook.' 'Ah!' exclaimed the first participant. 'But if you wrote it, you wouldn't make it boring.'

The challenge stuck and I talked later with other participants about it. They thought it was a good idea for me to write down what I teach. They didn't want one of those books with long lists of things you had to do to be a success. Lists so long that they took longer to read than implement. If you could remember by the end, the reason you started reading them, you were a genius. They didn't want neat diagrams. You know, the ones with the boxes, circles and arrows, always symmetrical with every word beginning with the letter 'P' or 'C'. They were fed up with the long case studies on famous multinational companies. Case studies saying how marvellous they were. One delegate said, 'if my company had as much money as they do and was as large as they are, I'm sure that some part of our business would be doing something right.' Another, on the same theme said 'what's the point in just telling us stories which we cannot copy? And anyway it's probably just as well we can't since they all seem to go off the rails eventually.'

Some of the managers on my programmes told me what they *did* want. 'What we want is a book which explains enough and then gives us enough of a pointer to get on with things.' 'What I want is a book that I can read and re-read until I have learnt the contents.'

So here it is. My first customer-driven book. I've tried not to be too boring. I've only allowed myself a few diagrams. I've only used a few cases directly although I've hidden and disguised a lot more. I've not name dropped a single multinational.

I hope it makes your life at work fun and helps with business too.

Eddie Obeng
Buffers End, Beaconsfield, U.K.
August 1994

ACKNOWLEDGEMENTS

I'll just make a list, in no order, of a small number of the people who have helped me write this book – my key stakeholders. I would like to say thank you to:

Richard Bach for reminding me what the purpose of life is.

Susan Obeng for letting me go, 'tap-tap-tap,' for hours on end, for worrying about me and making me express my thoughts more clearly.

Participants on my teaching programmes for the Idea and for turning a Fog into a Quest.

Garrison Keiller for making me laugh, and showing me how to write prose.

Jim Durcan for listening to my mad ideas and building on them.

Eli Goldratt for inspiring me with his masterpiece, *The Goal*. And for his marvellous conferences.

Carole Osterwiel for helping me with the glossary.

The Obengs and Roches for continually enquiring about progress.

Other delegates on my programmes for reading my manuscript and giving me feedback.

Emily, Sophie and Angela for inspiration.

My mum for keeping on at me.

Disclaimer

All the events in this book are entirely fictional. Any resemblance to any person or event is merely coincidental.

ALL CHANGE!

Chapter 1

FULL CIRCLE

I have been here before. Well, not exactly in this particular location, but in exactly this situation before. It's Monday. It's summer. It's very, very hot, and I have nothing to do but sit in the shade of a large red and yellow umbrella and try to understand why I am out of a job. This time it's the Mediterranean, the last time it was the Great Barrier Reef.

Friday was different. Friday was three days ago. On Friday I had a job, a responsible, well-paid job. Why, oh why had I quit? On Friday I had been convinced that I was right. Now I look down at the sand and say out loud, 'I was right. I know I was right.'

I play the scene through in my mind. I can hear Jane knock, open the door and come into the office. She's carrying a sheet of paper. I turn, look up at her and smile. She holds it out to me and I take it off her. I can see myself reading the memo. I can even feel my blood pressure rising, just as it had then. I grab at the phone and punch in numbers. A lady answers at the other end, singing, 'Infotech Solutions Limited, Hans de Vries' office, Jenny Jones here, how can I be of assistance?' I hear myself slam the door to my office behind me. I see the sunlit windows of the executive corridor flash by as I stride across the deep pile carpet. Usually I count them as I walk past, a habit I have developed over the years. This time I hardly notice them. I swoop through the door labelled 'Managing Director', past Jenny without saying 'Hello'. Suddenly I am standing in the middle of the office, leaning over the enormous walnut desk. I'm really mad. I'm ranting.

What has ended my 15 year career at Infotech Solutions Ltd, is the 'Go-For-It' Project. The title of the initiative had been dreamt up by Hans de Vries, our MD. He had attended a seminar on Total Quality Management. For him it was an evangelical experience. The very next day, he had called a seven o'clock breakfast meeting of the board. I was the only non-board member present. This was not unusual. As one of our firm's project leaders, I was often invited to crisis meetings. But this was different. There was no crisis, in fact business was going very well.

3

Hans had talked excitedly for about half an hour about how all our competitors were gearing up to 'eat our lunch' and that we could only look to the future with confidence if we went for it.

At this point he had turned towards me and asked me to spearhead something he described as 'Our organisational culture transfusion'. It is hard to be told that your organisation's future depends on you and *only* you and not be caught up in the hype. I had readily accepted. My job as project leader was to plan and control the implementation of a series of initiatives which would be championed by various board directors. I expected it to be a challenge but I didn't really understand what I was letting myself in for.

There were two real problems with 'Go-For-It'. The first was that no one at Infotech had the faintest idea how to change a culture. We didn't even really know what a culture was. I think that I learnt slowly as the project progressed. Although I learnt slowly, the rest of the organisation did not learn at all. It simply stayed ignorant. So steadily, a gap in understanding grew between me and everyone else. This gap made it more and more difficult for me to communicate with the senior managers in terms that they understood. They would argue with me over points which I felt were irrelevant to the progress of the project. I had to keep saying to myself over and over again, 'I *am* right, I *am* right, I *am* right.'

They didn't really understand many of the words I started using, such as **empowerment** and **process quality**. For example, they couldn't understand why I could not give them a progress report stating the percentage completion of the project. They were also concerned because there did not seem to be a long-term spend budget for the project; the main reason for this was that I would only propose spending money on items, such as training, once I had fully understood the need for it. And that tended to happen only when I felt that it was the way to make sure that progress would be made. This made it look, to senior management, as if I was out of control and making it up as I went along.

The second main problem was that, although no one would admit it, no one, including Hans, was really sure of the purpose of the project. Was it: to give us a better working environment; to improve product quality; to reduce running costs; to empower the staff; or was it something else? At every bi-monthly meeting it seemed to me that the steering group would invent a new purpose for the project. Some directors took advantage of this lack of clarity and launched initiatives, which they had been wanting to pursue for years, under the 'Go-For-It' banner, claiming it was in line with the objectives of the project. For example, the Personnel Director pushed through a new appraisal and review process. The process was very time consuming, especially for line managers. What was worse, in taking up so much time it was in direct conflict with another initiative on individual productivity and performance improvement sponsored by the Operations Director.

That was last year. Last Friday I stormed into Hans de Vries' office, thumped the desk and put forward an ultimatum insisting that I either got support from all the members of the board or I was leaving. He couldn't guarantee their support and now I was on a holiday of indeterminate length.

It really is great weather. The sea is a light greenish-blue colour which matches the sky perfectly. The sky is the same colour as Blue Curacao, the main ingredient of my favourite cocktail, *Blue Lagoon*, a concoction of lemon, vodka, and mineral water, poured over ice in a tall glass and coloured by adding an equal measure of the blue liqueur. I look towards the horizon and take a large sip and then return my mind to the problem I have been working on all holiday. I say to myself out loud, 'You keep repeating to yourself that you are right. If you *are* right then how come you are in this mess?' In my heart I knew that I had done the right thing but I can't really explain to myself how I have got to an end result which I haven't planned for and don't want.

I don't really understand and I never have. During twenty years in management, I had often been given responsibility for projects. The twenty years had passed quickly but not completely unnoticed. They were punctuated, stretching backwards, like poplar trees lining a long, straight, Roman road, but planted at uneven distances. There they were, my initiatives, my projects. It was supposed to always be the same. The excitement at the start of the project, the initial briefing, working out what was to be done, getting a team together, getting the bulk of the tasks done and then passing it over to the final users. But it never was. It was never as smooth as that; hiccups, backtracking, surprise grillings by senior managers, cash crises, late deliveries, concessions. Things always seemed to go wrong and I'd never really understand why and I still didn't. I'd asked other people and discovered that they were also mystified. It seemed that most people thought of it as a black art.

'The problem is that each project is different!' I'm talking to myself again. Along that twenty year journey, I must have attended dozens of one day courses and seminars on project management. I went in search of the Holy Grail. Usually what I took away was more like a plastic cup; a few good ideas and hints. 'They try to teach you a set of complex tools, usually to help with something like timetabling tasks or assessing risks. I can learn them, but no one else back at work understands what I am on about. And anyway, Murphy's Law means that it is pointless to rely solely on critical path assessments since all of the problems which come up are either unscheduled or are people problems.'

My mind wanders reluctantly backwards over my time at Infotech. The last time I almost resigned was over the Office Relocation. I am not enjoying recalling the past. I feel like an old soldier recalling the terrors of crossing a minefield in the dark without the aid of a mine detector. Frightened of blowing himself up or perhaps, even worse, being hit by the shrapnel from a mine set off by one of his platoon. Even now, after all those years, I still feel my palms dampen.

Office Relocation had been my first internal project. Unlike all the other projects at Infotech this was one we were doing for ourselves to ourselves. There was no outside client. There was no money to be made directly, only money to be spent. Spent on subcontractors such as the removals firm. The reason for the move was to reduce our costs by moving to a cheaper area, reducing the amount of office floor space and by reducing the number of individual offices we required. It was this; this second requirement which was the source of my problems. I'll never forget how my life changed when it was announced that I was to lead the relocation and would be responsible for all its aspects including office allocation and car parking. I instantly experienced an upsurge of popularity, for the following two weeks, I met and got to know more people in the organisation than I had during my previous six years.

There were two types of approach. I preferred the first, which basically constituted approaching me at the coffee machine or in the canteen, asking if I would be working late and offering to buy me a pint. Later, over a drink I would first be gently questioned (so that they could find out what the choice of office accommodation was). Next the conversation would switch to a long list of reasons, medical and non-medical, why such and such an office was an essential matter of life or death for my benefactor. Over the second pint, (also generously provided free), I would mumble an explanation that, 'things are still in an exploratory phase'. 'No decisions have been made yet.' and finally that,

'I can't promise anything but I will certainly bear them in mind when the time comes.'

The second approach was in no way subtle and was reserved for use by directors and senior managers. I would first hear on the grapevine that so-and-so was in no way pleased by something I was alleged to have done. I would then be urgently summoned to a meeting, in their current office (so I could see how palatial it was). I would arrive and be asked to wait, for at least fifteen minutes, by a stern looking secretary. Meetings were usually scheduled so that I would either see the MD going in or coming out of the director's office. I then had to sit through an hour long explanation of why this-or-that department was absolutely essential for the success of the organisation and listen to stories about how this-or-that department had saved the company from ruin many times in the past.

The other thing I recall from that internal project was that few people, if any, stuck to what they agreed in meetings or discussions. It seemed as if, not having written contracts, they felt free to do as they pleased, when they pleased. Once, I completely lost my temper with the Personnel Officer. He had promised to deliver lists of needs for our disabled staff. We needed the information in order to allow us to start the process of allocating space. Without it, we could make no progress with anything else. I called him up when the report was two days late and he flatly denied ever having offered any information. I flipped. I told him in no uncertain terms, both what I thought of him and exactly what I expected from him and by when, adding a description of how his widow would find him if he did not follow my instructions to the letter. The volume of my voice must have been tremendous, it had a similar effect to the trumpets at Jericho. The half height partition walls of my open plan office did not actually fall over, instead I found myself completely surrounded by sixty heads staring at me over their tops. I have never felt so embarrassed.

I finally solved the problems of matching people's actual needs, egos and status, by ignoring actual needs and simply ranking the offices by desirability and advantages and then matching them to our organisational chart. It wasn't perfect but at least it saved me from being lynched by everyone.

I had joined Infotech by accident. After my three months in Australia, where I had hung about and done exactly what I was doing now – nothing – I had returned to London. Two further months of aimlessness had broken my irresponsible spirit and I would have taken any job offered. As it was I had taken a job in the construction industry. An old school friend had suggested that I apply for a job as an assistant to a quantity surveyor he knew who was involved in a development in the city.

As assistant to the quantity surveyor, it was my job to ensure that everything went strictly according to plan from day-to-day. I had to make sure that there was no wastage in either tasks or materials. In practice this meant an eye for detail on just about every thing happening on the site. The complexity of the job amazed me. Individually the tasks themselves were simple enough but the complexity of the inter-connections between the architects, electricians, bricklayers, scaffolding experts, geologists, navvies and engineers were simply mind boggling. I began to appreciate that each of the skill groupings thoroughly understood their part of the task. They had, in fact, built up significant expertise by doing more or less the same thing on several previous projects. The difficulty with the building project was that it was large and complex and that their skills had never been used in that particular combination before. I enjoyed meeting and working with such a wide range of groups each of which seemed to have its own language and characteristics, from the navvies talking about, 'IG lintels' to the draftsmen with their 'Oh no! Not another rev!' which they would shout at any junior architect who walked into the drawing office.

In spite of that, the job hadn't suited me. Focusing on details and being mean are not part of my character and I found that after a while everyone seemed to have worked out a way of getting round me. My next move took me into information technology (IT). My move away from Property was caused by property, or to be more accurate, my landlord. My landlord had a son who was 'into IT' and over a lunch-time drink he mentioned that there were a number of jobs going in his company in what he called 'systems'. He seemed to think that with my academic background I would have no problem picking it up.

So I joined what was called Infotech Solutions Ltd. The business concept was to use information technology to supply business solutions to organisations. Our sales literature used the words Effective, Efficient, Productivity and Profit in all twenty-four combinations. The claim was that we helped businesses achieve these much desired states.

I'd been looking for a proper job. What I got was projects. I was given the title 'Assistant Systems Analyst', but in reality, at that time, our roles were not so well defined and I was more of a general dogs' body / trouble shooter / progress chaser. Chasing progress alone was a full time job. I spent the next two years hot on the heels of a series of projects which ran, ran and ran. In the end we nicknamed them *Locos*, (short for locomotives) to try to encapsulate the way in which they gradually gained momentum, shot off down the wrong spur of track, so that no one knew where they were, and with those on board finding them impossible to stop. My most vivid memory is that of the programmers constantly promising that since they were '90% of the way there they would only need another week to finish off the job' and insisting that there were 'only a few bugs to find and sort out'.

When, eventually, the day of unveiling finally arrived, without fail, a ritual would take place involving the end users, the ones who actually would have to live with the wizardry. As if working to a pre-written script, they would use the words 'slow', 'awkward', 'difficult'. This would be followed by expressions like 'once you get used to it' and 'why has the screen frozen?' After a suitable period of silence the users would decide that there had been much **change** but little **improvement** and would begin to demonstrate their ingratitude by insisting on a long list of modifications.

I look back over the sea. The sun has started its slow inevitable descent into the sea. In three hours it will be dark, a black sky studded with bright pinpricks of light. But it won't last, there is a gentle breeze already, a breeze which will eventually blow dark clouds across the sky, blocking out the light and covering up the clear view, backwards in time. I stand up and stretch. 'Isn't it funny that when you've seen it before, it is so easy to predict the future from so few clues. Shame it isn't the same with projects. If only I'd known at the start of each one what I knew by the end.' I sigh. If only we could predict the future and avoid the unpleasant bits. 'Ah well, that's life.'

But I'd tried to get a better understanding of what happened in projects. Over the years I'd also tried to discuss these problems with other project leaders. Though I thought that it was a problem, talking to them made it seem as if I was on my own. As a rule they tended not to confess to having any problems at all! Those who admitted to difficulties usually described them in the past tense. I understood their behaviour since I myself had often put on a brave and confident face as the only method of surviving disastrous projects. This made fellow project managers secretive about successes and failures and very difficult to learn from. That was another strange thing about managing projects, it wasn't like being a line manager. If anything at all went wrong all the fingers automatically pointed directly at you. The only aspect in which it was similar was that if things went right you could almost guarantee that someone else would get the credit.

Maybe I can work it out for myself? After all, I have lived through so many myself. 'Right, that's settled then. What was that quote?' I remember. *'Those who do not learn from the past are condemned to repeat it.'* 'By the end of this fortnight I really want to have understood how it all works.' I shall start off by looking back over my own experience.

I start to try to remember my past, always a difficult thing for me – I love the new, I love progress, I love pushing forward. I decide to think of myself after I graduated. I had taken two years off before going to University which meant that I was a very mature student. A bit old for employers who were looking for a fresh, bright, young graduate. Also, I don't think that my bushy beard and long hair helped much. So I was delighted when I was offered a post as a research assistant at the University. The money was not brilliant but I compared it to living on my student grant, and it felt as if it would support me in unparalleled luxury. The thought of being able to live in a heated flat again was too enticing and I'd accepted the post immediately.

I was to study the molecular structures of Soy proteins. The Green movement and Vegetarianism were growing, there was a need to develop meat substitutes. High protein soy beans could substitute. But once cooked, they smelt and tasted like beans and gave you wind. You couldn't make them into casseroles. At the time no one had a clue how to make vegetable protein taste and feel like meat. It was a challenge. If only you could, then you could make your million. Organisations were willing to pour money into studying molecular structures. This they thought held the key.

I was young. I'd dreamt of being a scientist. It looked exciting. And it was funded by two commercial organisations. The Confederation of Soya Bean Growers (usually abbreviated to CSBG) and KET Ltd., a heating equipment manufacturer. The bonus of being commercially funded was that I could sniff the scent of a real job in industry if all went to plan.

My boss was an egghead. At twenty-five he'd established the structure of a particularly tricky molecule using a piece of equipment he'd invented, designed and built. He was a tall, thin, arrogant, man with a bushy beard, called Costerly. Since he had the only, very expensive piece of equipment needed for the work, he was invited to lead the two year, quarter of a million pound project. The open goal of the project was to find out the right strains of soya bean to process on KET's equipment as meat substitutes. The Prof.'s hidden goal was really only to find an opportunity to use his equipment to study new and possibly Nobel prize winning molecular structures.

It was a terrible time. Demoralising and depressing years. Years spent repeating experiments, having to rely on often erroneous analytical results from a group of demotivated, demoralised, co-workers who were bored with the equipment and didn't understand the project goals. The boss did not communicate directly with us. I think he used telepathy to keep us all up-to-date and co-ordinated. Unfortunately none of us had the telepathic skills needed to receive his messages. He constantly invented new goals and experiments for us, and refused to take us seriously when we suggested that we were all more than slightly miffed at the way things were going.

Three years later, we'd spent four hundred thousand pounds, were one year late and, although we now had some very academically interesting micro graphs of molecular structures, we had no real information for our commercial sponsors. Well, what I mean is that we continued to call them sponsors although six months after the start of the project KET got a new managing director who didn't share his predecessor's enthusiasm for the project. And the CSBG was having difficulty maintaining the interest of its members. The year after we started was both warm and wet and the bumper crop which had resulted had led to a price war, prices had plummeted to a tenth of the previous year. Most of its members were either fighting each other or had given up the fight and simply gone bankrupt.

The Vice-Provost, who initially had seen the project only in terms of the financial benefits it offered, was not prepared for things going wrong. As the relationship with our sponsors deteriorated (the CSBG wouldn't pay up, and KET were threatening to sue us), he grew fatter and balder with every letter of complaint he received from KET or the Confederation about the lack of progress the project was making. He put more and more pressure on the Prof. to deliver. The Prof. kept us working on his agenda and simply used it as a way to put us under more pressure.

For me, it all came to a head one afternoon when I heard that Prof. Costerly had unilaterally cancelled a series of experiments I was planning simply because they didn't make use of his precious equipment. I hit the roof, told him that the project did not revolve around his 'stupid, expensive and trashy pile of junk' and described what he could do with his project. I was very graphic in my instructions. Later that day I bought a bucket shop airline ticket to Australia. It was the furthest I could get away for the least money. I really have come full circle.

Chapter 2

MY OLD MATE

It's been raining solidly for the past three days. Three days of horizontal rain striking against the window panes and then running down them in a thick uneven layer. A layer which makes the *Salon de Thé* sign on the building opposite appear to sway and dance gently and unpredictably backward and forward and the most annoying part of it all is that it shouldn't be happening. This is, after all, the South of France. By mid-afternoon I am bored with staring at the walls of my room. Staying on the beach is fine when it's sunny, you are a few minutes walk from restaurants, sand and other fun seekers. When the weather is not good, it's the pits! There is absolutely nothing to do. I decide to visit the local chateau which will at least be dry and will allow me to stretch my legs. It is there, wandering around the cellar, that I notice the shiny bald patch. You can hardly miss it. It shines or rather glistens, even in the cool darkness of the cellar. Then he turns round, and I slowly realise that I recognise the face belonging to the beacon. Instinctively and without having worked out who exactly I am about to address, I smile, and say 'Hello".

The eyes in the face stare straight into mine and with a smile of recognition he says 'G'day mate.' 'Did you ever find a job then?' A hand extends to meet mine in a warm, vigorous handshake.

His question answers my question, it is Franck. I had first met him at Surfers Paradise in Australia. He had also been on an 'extended holiday'. At the time he had just finished six years of studying psychological diagnostic techniques. We had become firm friends for the simple reason that both of us at the time were looking for some way of putting meaning into our lives. We had lost touch and I hadn't seen him for years.

I reply, 'Yes, eventually several but I've used them all up now.'

He says, 'What we need is a cold tube of beer, but would a glass of sparkling white wine do instead?'

I nod and point to the sign which says restaurant. In no time we are

13

reminiscing over the bad old times convincing ourselves that they were the best times of our lives.

I discover that Franck had also finally found a career, but now he works for himself. His description makes him sound like a supply teacher at a high school. He had described himself as an educator. It takes me about an hour to get round to the topic which has been on my mind all holiday. I tell him 'twenty years in projects, I've had some success with about half. What frustrates me is that I still haven't got a clue how to guarantee project success.'

He smiles at me as if I have said something really stupid, but says nothing.

I continue. 'I know that no one else has worked it out because they are all as surprised as I am whenever a project goes belly-up.'

He smiles again and it makes me feel that I need to put forward my theory on projects, so that he will not think that I am completely dumb. I have a voice I usually reserve for presentations to senior management. I call it my 'confident-bullshit' voice. I use it. I say 'Of course, projects go wrong because we don't push people hard enough.'

That smile again, and then he asks, 'So do you mean that you never have budget overruns from your team members claiming overtime?'

'Yes we do,' I reply 'but they only do overtime because we don't have enough control over what they do, and so they don't do what we need, when we need it.'

'Oh, I see!' he replies, 'Your fifty per cent success rate comes from projects where you have had a dedicated team over whom you have had total control.'

'No,' I insist, 'not quite.' We also need better planning tools and techniques.'

'I understand,' he says, and tops up my glass. 'What you are saying is that if only we could plan it all out in greater detail then it would all happen exactly according to plan.'

'I don't think you understand,' I say. 'Even with good plans, life just isn't like that, and,' I add, 'it takes years and years to become a decent project manager. It's very complex. You have to know how to do most of the jobs on the project, and all the methods and computer planning and control techniques.'

'I see. So you've never worked on a project for a mature, widely experienced project leader which has gone awry?'

I remember the building site and start to wriggle. 'Well, sometimes there are special cases,' I say.

For the first time in our conversation, Franck offers an opinion. What strikes me is the way in which he does it. His voice seems calm, deep and resonant as if he is speaking through a muted megaphone. He says, *'What I have found is that however complex the situation, it is unusual to find more than a half dozen underlying causes.'*

My instinctive reaction to any statement that I don't really understand is to argue with it in the hope that in discussion it will become clearer. 'I'm not sure I agree,' I say. 'This is a really thorny problem which has taxed many of the best minds for a long time.'

Franck says nothing but simply smiles, with much too much confidence.

I say, 'Maybe it can't be solved. Maybe there is nothing special which guarantees project success. It could just be luck.'

He smiles again and insists, 'I don't think you really believe that or you would not have started this conversation. So what do you think is the real cause of project failure? . . . and anyway what do you mean by failure? Explain it all to me. Start from the beginning.'

Chapter 3

HOLDING ON TO YOUR GAINS

'So what do people say once it's over?' asks Franck. He's stopped smiling now and looks at me as if he is hungry for a meal. He seems so serious over the problem that I get the feeling that he thinks that the meal is going to be me.

'It depends on who you ask,' I reply. 'The classical measures of project success are Time – Cost – and Specification. The client is usually most concerned with the first two whilst the end user is usually most interested in specification. That is, "does it do what we intended it to do for us?" However, I find more that these days for **business projects**, clients are often as interested in **revenues** as costs. The additional revenue from a new product development can often far outweigh the costs. Also clients are more interested in the **timeliness** than time itself. To use the new product example again, as long as they beat the competition to the window of opportunity, the exact timing is not as important as its timeliness.'

I plough on in a steady stream. 'But there are other groups of people who also have comments to make about project success. The person or steering group which owns or sponsors the project usually has a view. Their measure of success is usually in relation to them. Deciding how much political hassle it has been to push the project through? Furthermore, there is the project team, who try to assess whether they enjoyed the experience and would be willing to go through it with the project leader again. The accountants, who are still upset because you didn't spend, on what you said you would, when you said you would. And then there are the senior managers, whose noses are put out of joint because you have crossed into their patch unknowingly and they are determined to kill your project stone dead.'

'Whoa! Slow down, slow down,' he says, waving his arms up and down. 'It seems to me that lots of people hold a stake in the project.'

'Well yes but the *only* important one is the client, as long as we can keep the client happy . . .'

'You just told me,' says Franck steadily, 'that sometimes when you are half way through a project suddenly, out of the blue, you have received an angry or aggressive memo or a rocketing from some senior manager or union official or someone else who you thought had nothing at all to do with your project?'

I'm thrown by the question. I'm sure I didn't mention the rude memos. How does Franck know about them? The answer to his question is yes. Yes. Frequently. It's a horrible feeling, just as things are getting going on the project, out of the blue, like a bolt of lightning, it strikes you. It leaves you disoriented, annoyed and confused, and not wanting to read memos or answer the phone for a while. They usually start 'I have just heard...' And if you don't handle them right they will fight you and obstruct you for the rest of the project. I reply softly, 'Yes.'

He probes. 'Why does this happen?'

'I don't know.' I reply perplexed. 'I guess, they seem to think that the project is something to do with them.'

Franck continues to probe. 'How does this same thing happen over and over and over?'

'Busybodies?' I venture.

'I don't think so,' he says flatly. 'Go back to what you said before.'

'What?' I ask. 'You mean "*that they think that the project has something to do with them*"?'

He nods. 'Yes and what do you think?'

'That it doesn't,' I say slowly, as I begin to understand his point.

'And who's right? He pauses and waits for a reply from me. I know he's right but don't reply. Eventually he continues. 'It seems to me that there are a lot of people who have a stake and there are even more than you think.'

'Yes.' I agree, 'There are a lot of *stakeholders*. I sometimes feel like Dracula's assistant, constantly watchful and alert, trying to avoid an army of vampire killers who are determined to drive a stake through the heart of my project.'

Franck laughs and calls the waiter over.

'Yes,' I say thoughtfully, 'you're definitely right. There are a lot of stakeholders. Some have a financial or organisational stake in the **outcome**. For example, the client or sponsor who is actually paying for the project is the person who is really **driving** the change. They tend to drive it towards the outcomes they want. Other people may be

17

interested in the outcome but they may not be in the driving seat. For example, the sales department, which will grow as a result of the project, are betting on you to succeed. However the people who will lose out as a result of the project also have a stake and wish for you to fail.'

'Are some stakeholders more concerned with what happens during the project than the outcome?'

'Who do you mean?'

'How about the ones who are holding and steadying a ground stake for you to hit?'

I look at him completely puzzled.

'Your team, I mean,' says Franck.

I nod vigorously. 'And all the favours I need to call in, from across the organisation.' 'It's when you need to rely on work from people over whom you have no responsibility or authority, that you realise something which is probably true for every stakeholder.'

'What's that?' He asks.

'It also seems that some people are more interested in the **softer** measures of **how** things are done rather than the **harder** measures of **what** is done. Receiving favours, generating motivation and enthusiasm are far more dependent on how you dealt with people last time round. Did you share the whole vision with them so that they could understand where their contribution fitted in? Did you thank them? Did you make them do pointless work? Were your instructions useful and clear? How you worked with them has a far more profound impact on them, than informing them that the project or the tasks are going along to time, cost and quality.'

Franck leans across the table to fill my glass, as he does this that hungry look comes over his features again, and in a firm voice he repeats the question he had asked me five minutes earlier. 'So?' he asks conspiratorially, 'what do people say once it's over?'

With my new insight I reply, speaking slowly, to make sure I get it right. 'There are many stakeholders with different success criteria. However they fall into three groups. Some focus on the tasks delivered by the project and look at the hard and tangible outcomes in order to establish how they and the business will be affected by the change. In a business context their concern is with the *financial contribution* of the project, its *timeliness in providing competitive advantage*, and whether it delivers the *specific technical and business objectives it was set up for*.

Others are primarily concerned with the way in which they are managed, influenced and involved **during** the project. This group, responsible for delivering the change, usually involves the core team, all the other direct and indirect contributors to the project (including external suppliers and subcontractors). They are measuring success against their own *personal feelings, levels of motivation* and the *learning* and *development* that they get out of the project. In most modern projects this group is far more important than you might think because you usually have to work with them again in the future and they can have a significant influence over the rest of your career by actively or passively preventing you from succeeding the next time round, or simply by bad mouthing you to future teams and as a result, making it difficult for you to get their enthusiasm.

The third group are primarily concerned with *both* the outcomes of the project and how well they think that they have been managed during the project. Usually this group includes the client, end users and the project sponsor or steering group. For them, success is a measure of how all their expectations, both **hard** and **soft** have been met throughout the project.'

'Good', says Franck, 'so now we know what you are trying to avoid in projects. But that's only the first step, now we need to work our way backwards systematically to find out what skills or knowledge that all project managers lack, or let's be generous, which they fail to use consistently.

Let's start by trying to understand the business part of the problem. So, tell me, what do you think is the most common cause of problems with timeliness, money or specification?'

'I don't think that it is as simple as that,' I reply, trying not to show my surprise at how naive he seems to be. 'If there is one cause then I would say that it is the lack of planning.'

He looks straight at me and says provocatively, 'So what you are telling me is that all well-planned projects deliver the three business requirements?'

An image flashes through my mind. It is the image of my second ever project, the one on the construction site. I remember the portakabin where we had our tea breaks on rainy days. The cabin had been about thirty feet long and about ten wide. All the way round the walls at two levels three feet high there had been a band of steadily yellowing paper, our project plan. I remember someone telling me that it had taken a year to work out in detail all the tasks that had to be carried out and the order in which they had to be done. When I saw it, it was already one year out of date, the tasks we were working on bore no relation to what was on the wall. Many of the tasks which were represented as being one-offs we had in fact done several times over either because we made mistakes in carrying them out or because they had been wrongly specified in some way. We had had plenty of planning but once things started to go wrong they had simply gone from bad to worse and it had been impossible to keep the plan up to date with the changes.

I finally reply. 'No. And furthermore, even with excellent plans something unforeseen may occur. You need to know the status of the project all the time and be able to catch up or change your plans. This can be made even worse by tasks which are done wrong or have to be repeated to meet specifications.'

'You've given me four common causes, are there any more?'

'Yes, there is one more, the original financial or duration estimates may have been wrong or the specifications very demanding or unachievable, so that when you deliver the possible you are still seen to have failed.'

Franck takes a pen out of his top pocket and starts to make notes on the napkin. He writes:

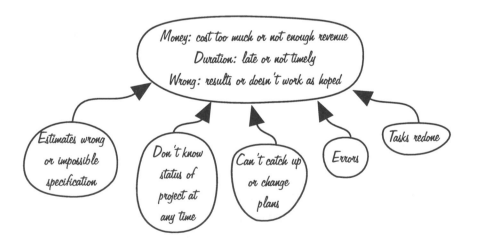

'What are you doing?' I ask.

'Blowing bubbles,' he replies, and without pausing, continues, 'on projects where tasks are repeated often, what else happens?'

'You mean apart from being late and overshooting on budget?'

'Yes,' he confirms.

I explain. 'The people working on the tasks get fed-up. If they get bored, as well, then their attention to detail tends to decrease and as a result they make more mistakes. All the people waiting to receive the outputs of the tasks become impatient. Their confidence in what is to be produced by the project starts to fall. They may lose interest in the project all together or it may fall down their priority list. If the task is for the client and it is redone several times, this is often enough to turn the client off you and it may become impossible to win future business.'

He looks up at me from the napkin he has been writing on and asks, 'Does this happen often?'

'Yes,' I reply, 'all the time.'

Franck writes '*team?*' and '*contributors fed-up*' and then adds two arrows to his scribbles, one from *tasks redone* to *contributors fed-up* and one from *contributors fed-up* to *errors*. 'Do you find that once a team starts redoing tasks all your plans get increasingly out of control?' he asks me.

'Yes,' I reply, 'sometimes the only way to overcome the problem is to change the people involved. How do you know about that problem?'

'Just a hunch,' he says cryptically. 'Tell me, what else do your two groups of stakeholders say at the end?'

Realising how much I have gained from the last ten minutes, how much the pieces are starting to come together, simply because I have more fully defined the needs of the organisation, I am thoughtful as I answer. 'Well, you can end up with an unhappy or demotivated project team. By project team I mean my core team, who help me run the project and are very closely associated with it, the working team made up of those who are supposed to be working on the project and all those people whose goodwill I have relied upon.'

'You mean your invisible friends?' he says.

I laugh at the idea, 'I suppose you could call them that! It's a great title. Just like childhood when your parents couldn't see your invisible friend, but you could and you knew what they were up to all the time. I definitely agree.' I giggle. 'Let me introduce you to my army of invisible friends. Meet . . . *The Invisible Team*.'

Franck grins. The waiter sidles up to us, in as obvious a fashion as possible clears his throat and demands, in French, 'Are you ready to order yet?' For the first time in four hours I notice our surroundings. It looks as if all the day trippers have left. The other clientele are dressed for an evening out. I turn back to face Franck who shrugs.

He rises from his chair and says, 'Just let me make a 'phone call and then maybe we can stay on and grab a bite to eat.'

Whilst he's gone I try to use the time to prepare for the next part of our discussion. I'm enjoying the way it's going. To be honest, I'm rather surprised at the interest he has taken in my problem. I've always thought of it as a rather specialised problem. I had not expected anyone unconnected with projects to have had the slightest interest. After all, Franck was only a teacher, or what was it he called himself, an 'Educator'?

I notice the napkin he's been scribbling on and reach across the table to pick it up. 'What a crazy way to make notes,' I think. The diagram is untidy. It looks like a pile of spaghetti. Arrows cross each other, one set goes round in a circle. I follow the arrows of the circle round, reading the words out softly to myself, '*Errors → tasks redone → team fed-up → reduced attention to detail → errors.* What on earth does that mean?' Then I remember Franck's question, the one which had surprised me, and my answer.

He'd asked. 'Do you find that once a team starts redoing tasks all your plans get increasingly out of control?'

And I had replied 'Yes. Sometimes the only way to overcome the problem is to change the people involved. How do you know about that problem?'

'The sly goat!' I jerk my head up. 'So that's how he knew.' I had told him myself. He obviously has some shorthand way of writing down what I say and then pieces it all together and feeds it back to me. Of course, if errors lead to tasks being redone and redone tasks lead to the team getting fed-up, and a fed-up team tends to pay less attention to detail then this will lead to more errors being made. Once that starts it's obvious that it'll snowball, getting steadily worse. That was just typical of Franck, always pulling a fast one of some sort.

Just then he returns to the table and sits down. I'm restrained, not eager to let him in onto what I have just discovered. He notices the napkin in front of me and asks, 'Trying to decipher my hieroglyphics?'

'I think I may have made some progress,' I reply, but I can't resist asking, 'how does it work?'

'We've only just started,' he says. 'I'll explain it later when we have made some real progress.' Then he looks at me in an apologetic way.

'I'm afraid that the explanation will have to wait though. I have to go and can't stay for dinner. Maybe we can meet again?'

Chapter 4

A PANACEA WHICH CAN MAKE YOU ILL

I come off the 'phone. It has been an expensive call. A peak time call to the UK. I hadn't wanted to make it, but after all I am out of work and I need to look for another job and the only time that I can call to follow up the applications that I have put in for jobs is during working hours, UK working hours. The particular application I am following up is a reply to an advert in the Sunday Times from a small consultancy firm asking for 'Change Consultants'. I don't really know what a change consultant is. But the description of the job sounds a lot like some of the project management jobs that I have done in the past. I've always been a bit of a smooth talker and I'm convinced that as long as I can get in for an interview I stand a good chance of convincing them that I am the right person for the job.

The reason the call took so long was that I had been trying to reach the senior partner but had been sent around in circles. I had started off with a receptionist. I had explained who I was and why I needed to talk to the senior partner, she had put me on hold, then I had gone to a secretary, junior consultant, back to the receptionist, a partner, the admin. manager, back to the receptionist and finally to the senior partner's secretary who informed me that she was out but would probably wish to speak to me and could I try again later. This was rather lucky for me, because by this time I am afraid that I had completely run out of patience and was not sure if I actually wanted the job any more.

What had infuriated me was that each time and with each person I had had to go through my entire explanation. It seemed that they were incapable of passing on simple messages to each other! What would they have done if I had been a client? In the middle of a project, a team incapable of communicating, cannot function.

'Of course,' I exclaim, 'that is it! Communication. That, is the secret of project success.' It is so simple. I wonder why I had forgotten to mention that to Franck yesterday, but now it is so obvious to me. I am surprised that he had not suggested it himself. And being a teacher, or what was it he calls himself? an *educator*; surely that's what he does for a living?

It's hard for me to think of Franck as a teacher, a respectable member of the community. In my mind Franck was still the good-time anarchist that he had been twenty years ago. At the time his main interests were beer, beer, and solving the world's problems. He could make us laugh for hours by the way he would take a really serious problem like world hunger, turn it on its head and come up with crazy solutions. One of his solutions for that was to brand food aid, not from the country it came from, but by the politician who had ensured that it be sent. So for example you could have Richard Nixon corned beef hash, in cans complete with a photograph of Tricky Dicky on the side and a quotation from him. Or you could have the Harold Wilson instant milk powder, just add water and stir. Knowing how shallow and egocentric politicians are, they would compete fiercely to try to get their face seen by as many of the starving as possible. The problem would thus be solved overnight.

I'm sitting on the sofa in the front room of my apartment. It is a bright room and feels more like a home than a holiday chalet. It even has pictures on the walls. Opposite is a Monet painting of poplar trees. Fantastic these impressionists, at this distance it looks very real and solid but I know that it is made up of mixed-up, small patches of unconnected colour. Above the mantelpiece there is a Tolouse-Lautrec poster of a woman dancing the can-can. It is painted in bold colours. The dancer's name is Jane Avril. I know her name because it is written across the poster, which was originally designed for advertising hoardings. I sit there wondering how a person, who can sink so many beers, could possibly manage students. Thinking about students and Franck reminds me of my university research job. The job I had just left when I first met Franck. I feel my chest tighten as it used to from frustration. Isn't it strange how, after all these years, I still have not gotten over the experience. The reason I feel uncomfortable is that I remember him, my boss, the telepathic academic.

I remember how every new development had been a complete surprise to the whole team and how little we knew or understood about what was going on overall. I remember how the sponsors, KET and CBSG, had been just as surprised as we had by each twist and turn in the project.

I say out loud to myself 'Communication is most definitely the key! Projects fail because there is not enough communication'. Franck had said that there were no more than half a dozen causes. He had over-estimated. There was really only **one** underlying cause.

I smile and lean back in my chair. I feel so good about my conclusion that I have stopped feeling the pain of 150 Francs wasted on an inconclusive 'phone call. There is nothing quite like feeling a genius to anaesthetise the aches and pains of life. Then, slowly, with the same dull feeling that you get at the start of a headache, I begin to feel uncomfortable about the conclusion I have just reached. I think, 'if a lack of communication is the main cause of project failure, then there won't be any 'failed' projects, where the project leader does lots of communication.'

Oops!' I think, 'a small problem.' I remember the early projects at Infotech. The ones which we had called *Locos*. Each project had had a different project leader and since I was often working on more than one at a time I'd had a good opportunity to compare the styles of the different project leaders. Now in retrospect, I try to remember particular details about their communication styles. I allow images of these leaders to swim into my mind, along with my initial image of Professor Costerly, and try to classify what they did. As it turns out I don't have to think too long. The very first image completely disrupts my original conclusion. A conclusion that I'd based on a hunch and tried to make truth with one example. An example based on the Professor. The image which is causing the discomfort is five foot six, wears glasses and travels at a tremendously high speed down corridors. It is of Audrey Peters.

Audrey had led one of Infotech's first, book-keeping automation projects. Audrey had really believed in communication, '*The more the better*,' she believed. She kept us all up-to-date with daily briefings and weekly meetings We were all obliged to attend the daily briefings. The problem was not with the briefings themselves. They were true to title. They were brief. The problem was that little of what was covered was of any relevance to three quarters of the people who were briefed. In practice our brief had little to do with the broad spread of our daily activities, and made little difference. Because they were so frequent, the overall position of the project was never discussed and as a team member I had little idea of the bigger picture. The weekly meetings followed exactly the same formula, except in one respect. True, they were weekly and true we met. True too that meeting had little to do with what we did apart. And true they focused only on detail. The real difference was that they were tremendously boring.

Audrey's formula for get-togethers, it seemed, was to make sure that we were provided with as many facts and as much data as was available, even if it did not answer any of the day-to-day questions which we faced. Audrey was also a great one for circulating memos, which she had been sent, to the whole core team and any of the members of the invisible team whose names she remembered whilst drawing up the circulation list. In my early days on the project I used to have to take the circulars home and read them in the evening to keep the 'in' tray at less than the maximum two inches which would fit into the slot. Eventually, I learnt that the trick to surviving the paper deluge was to scan the document quickly, looking down the 'action column' for your initials. If they were absent the document could be ticked off and circulated. Anyway even if you failed to spot your initials you were certain to get a personalised copy as a reminder, sooner or later.

I glance down at my watch. 'Damnit!' I'm going to be late. I've been happily day-dreaming and now I'm going to be late for my appointment with Franck. I hate being late. Over the years I've gotten to feel worse and worse about being late. Especially with project work. I guess it's because it's so obvious to everyone if you're late. If you're late, they can tell that you're failing. It's much more difficult to hide than cash over-spends or not meeting specs. And anyway the hard criteria of success are of an order of magnitude harder to hide than upsetting or falling out with your stakeholders. It's very easy to hide the poor state of the relationship which you have with your stakeholders and anyway, you can always claim to be getting on famously.

I check my hair in the mirror by the front door, open the door and head out towards the car. As I am passing a petrol station I glance at the fuel gauge to check if I have enough fuel. It reminds me of my earlier thoughts. Too much detailed factual data. Unsorted factual data not aimed at anyone in particular. Certainly not aimed at me. No answers to the questions that I had. Not enough of a view of overall progress. Audrey's The project still ended up a *Loco*, coming in eventually a year late and 120 per cent overspent with a fed up team and an unhappy client.

What I conclude from Audrey and the Professor was that, what was important about communication was not 'how much' but whether *it serves the purposes of the **person being communicated with***.

27

As I drive along, I know that I still do not have the full picture. So I continue to work through my list of project leaders I have known. In particular I think about Bob Timson. Bob had joined Infotech from one of its equipment suppliers, three months before I had. I suspected that he had been on a management course which had stressed the need for interpersonal communications. He excelled at this. His style was one-to-one communication. He would seek you out and discuss issues at great length if he had the full details. If he did not have the full details, he would simply make them up.

The process was exactly the same if you needed information or a decision. There was masses of communication, usually focused on what you were trying to achieve. Sometimes explaining where things had got to in terms of the bigger picture; but most of it was wrong or unclear. When it was wrong it was wrong because in trying to be the font of all knowledge he would be overgenerous with the truth. When it was unclear it was because he always communicated at such a level of detail, that it was as if he was providing you with detailed instructions of what your job required, in a minute-by-minute, step-by-step fashion. This would have been fine, if he actually understood the nature of the job and had grown up in it, but since he had a manufacturing background he did not. As a result he gave a patchy, confusing and inappropriate message.

So to communicate successfully *you need to send out messages **which are correct***. There is also a need to decide how much detail the person you are communicating with can handle. The *core team may require the **full details** whilst the sponsor or senior client may only wish to know the top level of the **bigger picture. Providing detail when an overview is all that is needed is as bad as doing it the other way round***.

And then there was Patrick Phelan, the man who 'snatched defeat from the jaws of success'. It had looked as if Infotech was about to net a real success. The client thought we were marvellous and had even started recommending us to other prospective customers. Team morale and spirit were high, a thing I have rarely seen. Project team members actually knowing their individual roles but also bending over backwards to help each other and to fill in any gaps, in roles, that arose as the project progressed. Most of the team members were only working on the one project rather than the normal practice of being spread over several projects.

Unfortunately, Hans de Vries, our MD, had another one of his brilliant ideas. The timing of the idea was also unfortunate since it coincided with the closing stages of the project and occurred before it had ended completely. At the board meeting in March of that year, he announced that full time members of all projects would only be retained by the organisation at the end of the project, provided there was another project for them immediately to join. Joining another project team would not be automatic. Even if there were vacancies, the person would need to put a strong case, which was supported by the project leader of the project that they intended to join.

Pat learnt of this new policy from his copy of the minutes of the board meeting. It must have hit him hard because he decided two things. Firstly that it was very bad news and secondly that the best way to get rid of bad news is to dilute it. This you do by telling as many people as you can as quickly as you can. Pat did a marvellous job at communication. First he called us together and explained the company's circumstances. He then explained the implications for all the projects that were running and went through the details of the policy, finally asking us each to consider what the implications were for us. He then sent us round a mcmo summarising what had been covered. I believe that he actually had meant to help and reward us for our loyalty throughout the project. He knew that we had worked hard and did not want us to suffer by losing our jobs. I think he felt also that it was a stupid policy and wished to place the blame for its impact, fairly and squarely where it belonged; with the MD.

He had done an excellent job of communicating to us, which meant that we all understood what was at stake. Everyone on the project immediately started to plot, wheel-deal and scheme to move to other longer term projects, as soon as possible. People with little left to do on the project let it drag out, making deliberate mistakes to give themselves more time to find a place on another project. Morale collapsed, since some of us were in direct competition with each other for future jobs, and the less scrupulous began to look for opportunities to denigrate the work being done by others. There was also some subtle sabotage. From the team's point of view it was an immense success. Ninety-five percent of us stayed on with the company having managed the shift.

The project of course turned overnight into a disaster. The 5 per cent we lost was Patrick. Four months later he had had enough, and quit.

*The **timing** of **communication** can seriously affect its usefulness. To communicate effectively you must **anticipate** the **thoughts** and **actions*** *you expect the person being communicated with to carry out.*

As I round the bend I see a lorry pull out from a side road. I bring my fist down, hard, on the steering wheel. 'Ten more kilometres. Now I'm really going to be late.' I can see that I'm at the point at which the slope of the road is starting to get steeper. I shrug my shoulders and resign myself to the inevitable. I say to myself, 'Relax. After all you are on holiday' and then I go back to my problem.

The final project manager who swam into view was Oswald Micheson. The two things that struck you about Oswald were his height and his vanity. He wore his hair in a coiffured bouffant style all piled up above which made his four foot eleven seem more like five foot seven. He had started his career in sales. My theory was that he had never really got the hang of selling and that was why he had ended up in projects. Anyway, somewhere along the way, he had acquired the looks and attitudes of a second rate estate agent. He was smarmy and slimy and had acquired the habit of saying things he thought sounded good. Statements like; 'This is a really exciting project' and 'I am committed to delivery on time' and 'Sticking to our budget is essential' were frequently used. There was however one small problem. The context within which he made these pronouncements. It didn't really work. Saying, 'This is a really exciting project' without any hint of interest or excitement in his voice, or 'I am committed to delivery on time' whilst always turning up late for meetings, or 'Sticking to our budget is essential', whilst filing yet another enormous expense claim, just did not send out a coherent message. We soon learnt to watch what he did rather than listen to what he said.

In particular the women on the project hated and distrusted him. They said that he made their skin crawl. He could make my skin crawl also. Whenever he was being particularly insincere he would adopt a very softly spoken tone. He used this soft and breathless voice whenever he wanted to drive a point home.

*To communicate effectively you must be **credible** to the person you are communicating with. **Everything you do must mirror** the **message** that you are trying to communicate. People watch closely what you **do** and use this as a far more reliable guide to what you **really** mean.*

I look at the lorry in front. It is filthy and puffing out ominous black clouds of smoke as it makes its way gradually up the hill. The logo on the back is a yellow arrow threaded through interlinking circles and squares. There is a line of text below the logo. The text is covered in grime. I work to try to read what it says. It's a challenge. After two attempts I think I have it. It translates roughly as 'No matter what the obstacles, weather, or route, we get your goods from here to there.' I snort as I realise, 'Communication is **not two** way. It is a **one** way process' A one way process fraught with difficulty. You need to deliver the goods. And the person being communicated with needs to confirm that they're the right goods. But even the journey back is just as difficult. In everyday life this is bad enough but in projects where things only happen once, and are not repeated day-in day-out, it is essential to get that one way trip right each and every time.

As I pull into the car park, I feel quite good about my reasoning, although it is clear that I still have some way to go to work out how communication fits into the picture. It certainly is important but now I know that it is not *the* key.

Chapter 5

BUBBLE No 1
LEARNING TO LEARN

It's a magnificent sight, St. Tropez harbour. The sea is still and an azure, milky, blue. The contrast of this dull background and the bright sunlight makes the colour of the yachts even more vivid and even through my very dark glasses the speed boats and yachts glow brightly. There are some truly magical vessels. They range from the low graceful sloops with their double masts to the thoroughly modern ocean-going yachts, painted in black and white several stories high. These floating palaces have been designed so that even when stationary, they seem to be travelling forward at a tremendous rate of knots. A trick of the light, well captured on the drawing board, a method of making the stationary look mobile. The same trick used in cartoons, to make vehicles appear to be travelling forward, by understanding the impact of parallax on movement.

Ours is a far more modest affair. It looks stationary when it is. It had been Franck's idea. It was to make up for rushing off before our meal two days previously. I had explained to him that I was certain that my meagre finances would not stand any major expense but he assured me that he had a good friend, a 'brain mate' as he described her, who owned a small yacht which he was sure we could borrow. The idea was to make the crossing to the small Island of Hyres. We were then planning to climb to the top of the main mountain and picnic.

Now we sit at the top of the hill, watching the boats below us carry out a complex waltz. The sunshine is hot but up here on the hill the blustery wind keeps us cool. Franck takes a copy of today's *Le Monde* out of the basket and spreads it on the grass. He then proceeds to empty out the contents of the picnic basket onto it. When he has finished setting out our lunch, he sits down, pours out two glasses of wine, turns to me and says, 'Well?'

'Yes,' I reply, 'very well indeed.' I smile broadly and say 'Excellent in fact.' I misunderstand his question on purpose. He knows how impatient I am and thinks that I will not wish to lose any time at all in resuming our discussion.

'Look,' he says, and points to a boat which looks as if it has dropped its anchor about a mile offshore. There seem to be people standing on a low platform on the end of the boat. 'Divers.'

I can make out six figures. Three of them have red tubes on their backs. The red tubes are actually cylinders. 'Oxygen cylinders,' I think, 'they are deep sea diving.'

'There is a wreck out there. The thing with wrecks is that they stick strictly to Murphy's Law.' He turns towards me. 'Once sunk they seek out the deepest part on the surrounding sea bed and wedge themselves in as deep as they can go. Even when the average depth is a few feet, any wreck in the area is bound to be at least a hundred feet down. When they are really deep, you can only get down to them with the aid of oxygen and sometimes it takes several dives to unearth all the secrets. You and I have probably got enough time this afternoon for one good dive to the bottom.'

I look at him puzzled and ask, 'What do you mean? I'm not a very good swimmer.'

'No.' He laughs. 'Not in the sea, I mean dipping into your problem with projects.'

'Oh yes,' I say, 'I must confess that I am very surprised that you are interested in the topic.'

He turns away from me. A second passes, then he stares back at me and says, as if he is about to offer me the challenge of a lifetime. 'Look at this,' he holds up a pot of low fat prune yoghurt. 'Think back ten years, and imagine yourself in a supermarket walking past the yoghurt section.' I nod, listening intently. He continues in a firm voice, 'What flavours of yoghurt were there?'

I'm not sure if he seriously wants me to answer and I hesitate. He keeps looking at me with the little white pot held up at eye level and I realise that he is serious. I don't understand the mismatch between his serious expression and this trivial question. I smile with relief and reply 'That's easy, plain and Strawberry.'

'OK, smug face, then try this one. Imagine yourself in a supermarket today, in the yoghurt section. What flavours are there?'

'I can't tell you that,' I retort, 'there are hundreds of them, and there are different types; French set, Greek, thick, live!' My arms circle in the air to illustrate the endless ranges.

He continues calmly 'And tell me what happens when you find one that you really like, say rhubarb, kipper and walnut flavour.'

'They change it or withdraw it.'

'Life is *all change* these days,' states Franck. 'All through the ages people have thought that. I remember my grandfather complaining about how much change there was, how much more complex it all was. He would moan about how much more renewal of everything from houses to pubs to forms of transport there was than when he was younger. It could just be something we feel as we get older but this time I think it is completely different. I think *change itself has changed*. Let's just stick to the yoghurt. The type of change we see these days is less of a step change and more of an alteration. We are less likely to see a step change – a change from no yoghurt to suddenly inventing yoghurt. We are more likely to see alterations or slight modifications.'

I nod in agreement. 'Even with technological change; computers were invented years ago. It's just that they keep getting smaller and more powerful.'

Franck continues talking softly as if speaking to himself. 'This time I think that it really is different,' he reiterates. 'I think that there are four things which happen today which didn't really happen in the past. These three seed changes have altered the way in which the world functions. It's the same world only the rules and formulae which govern it have changed. A bit like moving from water into wine,' he says as he tops up his glass with water. 'Both are liquid but they are not the same.'

I'm trying to follow him. But I need more clarification so I ask, 'What are these seed changes?'

'I don't know about you, but I can't remember the last time I met anyone from **any** organisation which is not *actively pursuing change*. Businesses, banks, governments, hospitals **all** seem to be trying to **change** things. And since *communications are now fast, global, relatively cheap and accurate*, customers and competitors world-wide hear of what they are up to. The competitors react by starting their own changes and the customers react by raising their expectations and being continually dissatisfied with anything they are offered. At the same time most *goods and services are having to rely on more technologies, skills and know-ledge to get produced and sold.*' Franck pauses in his monologue, looks out over the shimmering sea again and then he uses it. That tone again, the one which had struck me, the muted megaphone, to say, '*These* days, for most people life is all change.'

I'm not convinced so I press him, 'But,' I say 'you mentioned that your grandfather had thought the same, I can't see how this differs.'

'Remember the yoghurt?'

'Yes.'

'Imagine that the packaging has been changed. Doesn't the impact of that work its way down the chain to the printer who could be anywhere in the world? And then to the person who supplies the ink who could also be anywhere in the world is instantly faxed a note cancelling orders. It works its way then to the company which supplies the raw materials for the ink who see the demand for their product fall and so launch a sales push which soon gets their competitors anywhere in the world to launch their own.' He delivers this at a fast pace. 'And because the packaging was changed you didn't buy your yoghurt, so somewhere out in the North Sea a fisherman has a wasted catch which gets thrown back, adding to pollution at the same time. Because the fisherman didn't sell the catch he goes bankrupt, so he goes home to Iceland angry and beats his children. The children get taken into care and so the national budget is overspent so the country quickly has to increase it's borrowings. Interest rates change in America as a result and the stock market in Hong Kong moves.' Franck grins broadly.

I recover well from his machine gun delivery. 'You are trying to explain that change is less predictable, more complex and occurs at a faster pace.'

'It's more fragmented and surprising, so organisations find that they can't do it all at once. If the change you attempt is large, and a complete solution, you find that the benefits you were after slip through your fingers as the goal posts move. And you find that the act of trying to manage all the change as you would manage an organisation through a structure is much too difficult. In fact *the only way to stay ahead is to try to break the change you need to carry out into parcels or chunks and then to* **manage the change in chunks and hold on to your gains**. I am trying to learn as you are and I am interested in projects because they seem to be the most effective way of managing parcels or chunks of change. Don't forget that for years projects have been used to co-ordinate and manage changes of one sort or another.'

'Is that why you were giving me such a hard time on my theories of why projects went awry?' He doesn't reply so I continue to talk, 'Well,' I say 'I've been doing some more thinking and I figure that communication has a lot to do with it. I can't work out why it didn't come up the last time we spoke.'

'Didn't it?' He smiles that smile of his again and says, 'I don't really recall,' and reaches into his pocket. He pulls out the napkin he'd been scribbling on last time and smoothes it out on the top of the picnic basket. 'You're right,' he says, 'it's not on the napkin. Why do you think it should have been?'

'Because most people will say of their problems that they are *all down to poor communication*.'

'Well let's test this out. Why is the project not timely or why isn't the money going to be right or why doesn't it do what we expected it to?'

'Because there is poor communication?' I venture.

'That is a bit of a leap of faith. I'd love to see you sell that to your bank manager.' He then begins to act out, on his own, an interview with a bank manager. He is playing both parts.

He starts off as the bank manager. He crosses his arms and then looks up as if someone has entered the office. He then smiles and waves expansively to a non-existent empty chair, and says, in a nasal Oxford accent, 'Do sit down. What can I do for you?'

He shifts his position to face the place where he had been sitting as the bank manager, hunches his shoulders, trying to look intimidated, and says in a trembling high pitched voice, 'My project is late, overspent and not delivering the goods and I'd like to borrow £100,000 to improve my communications.'

He is the bank manager again. 'Could you please show me your business plan, to help me understand how the one thing leads to another? In what specific way will the fact that everyone knowing what everyone else is doing solve your problems with incorrect initial estimates or an impossible specification. Will it stop all errors being made?'

He moves round again, starts to wring his hands, looks up timidly and says, 'Well no, not really, but *everyone knows that it's all down to communication*.'

He stops acting and looks at me. 'Do you get the loan?'

'What do you think?'

He sticks out his lower lip, frowns slightly and shakes his head slowly from side to side.

'I see your point,' I say grudgingly 'but the visible and invisible teams could be demotivated because of poor communication, couldn't they?'

'Have you ever seen a situation where the project team was

demotivated and yet there was good communication?'

'Yes.' I say, remembering my thoughts of earlier that afternoon. 'So what you are saying is it's only in some situations that poor communication is a cause of team problems and in others it is not.'

'Let's work on the general case for projects first and build some patterns. Then we can look at specific cases, who knows, communication might be part of the solution.'

Franck looks back at the napkin and says, 'If I remember rightly there were three things which represented project success. One was to do with the actual content of the project, its timeliness, financial contribution and the specific technical and business objectives that it was set up for. The other two were to do with your, what did you call them again?'

'Stakeholders'.

'Ah yes, Stakeholders! The Visible and Invisible teams involved in its execution, and the stakeholders interested, primarily, in the outcome.'

'The sponsor, end users and client stakeholders.'

'The outcome stakeholders! I remember now,' he says, and then fixing me with his eagle look again he states, 'As long as you provide the expected goods to time and cost, I don't believe that in any project it is possible to end up with dissatisfied outcome stakeholders. How could this possibly happen?'

'It does happen.' I insist. 'I've seen it many times. I've lost future business or further phases of project work to competitors before now. More than once, would you believe. The final end user has refused to take advantage of the outcome of the project rubbishing it and being disparaging about the benefits and sometimes even sabotaging the project, just so that they can say, "I told you that it was no good". And I'll tell you why too!' I say, the pitch of my voice rising several octaves, 'It's because the outcome stakeholders never know what they want until it's impossible to give it to them.'

'But don't they tell you fairly early on in the project what outcomes they expect?'

'Yes they do, but they don't understand all the problems that I face and anyway they always each want an outcome which is different to everyone else's.'

'So what do you do if this is the case?' 'That they don't understand what they want or agree with each other.'

'I ignore them and hope that they will go away so that I can get on,' I reply sheepishly. Franck is giving me that fixed look again.

'So you can't really succeed.'

'Yes I can,' I insist, 'I've had several successful projects.'

'Have all your stakeholders agreed that they were successful?' He presses me for an answer.

'No.' I protest, 'But that is impossible.'

'What did we decide we meant by a *successful project?*' he demands.

I know that he's got me, so I don't answer, but I know he is right. *Project success is and can only be defined by the stakeholders.*

'So one reason that you've lost future business or upset your sponsor or failed to gain the ownership of the outcome by the end users, is that you haven't managed them during the project,' he states seriously. 'You'll have problems if you tend not to manage your stakeholders'

'Well I'd like to manage all my outcome stakeholders but you've never run a project, you don't realise how much there is to be done, I'm too busy to spend time trying to match up their whims. In fact I would often go out of my way to do as much as possible to keep the outcome stakeholders out of the action during the project,' I look at him and confide, 'it's the only way that you can really get on with things.'

'But tell me, don't they come back and bite your bum eventually, insisting, later on, on what they would have asked for earlier if you had given them the chance? And, isn't it worse for you when they finally get their say, later rather than sooner? Doesn't this mess up your half complete plans even more than it would have had you not ignored them?'

Franck is succeeding in being a totally annoying person. In theory he was right, of course, but how could he understand? This was the *real* world we were talking about. A world with fourteen hour working days and eight day weeks. How could I possibly find the time? I figure that being a teacher he doesn't really understand the pressures of real life. Well, with those long summer holidays. I'm trying to find a way of explaining how things are without being patronising, when he starts to speak. My mental state of mind must have been mirrored in the way in which I am vigorously applying my Roquefort to my baguette because Franck asks, 'When you are leading a project do you find that you get very busy?'

I stare at him in disbelief. Now I know that he is living in a different world. 'Are you kidding?' I say, 'It's all go, non-stop, sixteen hour days, rush, rush, rush, no holidays for months.' 'You're worn out but you keep driving, keep pushing, the adrenalin keeps you going.'

'What exactly are you doing?' he asks.

I spread my arms wide as a reply. 'Everything!' I exclaim.

'So you work **alone** on your projects then?'.

'No!' I shake my head. 'You don't understand. I am a project leader, I always have a team.'

'So how come you have to do everything?'

'I don't really have to do everything.' 'But I do need to be involved. It's the only way I can keep up to date.' I insist.

'If you were right, then this would not exist.' He pulls a sheet of newspaper from the copy of *Le Monde* we are using as a table cloth.

'Huh?'

'You said that the only way to keep on top of things is to be involved. Every day hundreds of millions of people keep up to date with the world's events without having to be personally involved in everything.'

'But I find it easiest to work out what is going on when I am involved.'

'So what you are telling me is that, one of the main reasons that you find yourself immersed up to your elbows in hands-on activities, is because, **you** *can only learn* **first hand** *about what is going on around you.*'

I shrug my shoulders 'Sure! That's how it is in the real world. That's how I am, there is nothing I can do about it.'

Franck smiles broadly and announces, 'At last the wreck has been found!'

I look over the bay, I squint and reach for my sunglasses. My eyes pan across the whole bay but I cannot see the boat with the diving platform. I turn to Franck and say, 'Where has the boat gone?'

'What boat?'

'The one with the divers. You said that the wreck had been found.'

'Oh! I was talking about *your* wreck. I meant that we had found **one** of the underlying reasons for your problems with projects.'

'When?' I ask, confused. 'I mean, how?'

He points to the crumpled napkin and says 'Do you remember that you told me that you often find that the client or end user claims that their requirements have not been met?' He points at the bubble which says this.

I nod in agreement 'Yes. I do.'

'You told me that you have difficulty in learning about things unless you are personally involved.'

I nod, and wonder where this conversation is leading.

He continues, 'That will give you two problems. The first will occur when you receive the briefings about the project. You hear what they say, but in your mind you instantly try to relate what they are saying to previous projects you have been involved in, accepting the parts which look or sound familiar and simply ignoring the bits that don't fit. You don't do this maliciously. It's quite simply that not having been involved in the problem that gave rise to the solution, the need for change, the change that the project is supposed to provide, the nuances and complexity don't mean much to you.'

'Go on.'

'What that means is that you may start a project without fully learning what your outcome stakeholders, and especially your client, actually wants.'

'How do you know this?'

'Do you ever find that after you have started, the goals feel less clear than they did at the start?'

'Mm, sometimes.'

'And do you ever find that you can carry on for a long time without feeling the need to review your goals?'

'Well, yes, but I have a lot of experience and I usually know what I want.'

'I know, but we have already agreed that what **you** want may not be what the outcome stakeholders want, even at the outset.' He is writing on the napkin again. 'If you are not reviewing your goals you will often find yourself wrong footed and, with infrequent reviews of the overall purpose, you may find it difficult to catch up or change your plans.'

I have to agree. I hated that experience which tended to happen about 90 per cent of the way through the project when, usually in an ad-hoc meeting or in a memo which you just happen to see, you discover that the stakeholders see a major problem and the terrible thing is that you know that you have not got enough time to put it right.

Franck carries on, he notices my bobbing head and assumes that I am with him. 'I said that there were two problems arising from your method of learning, the second is that you will almost certainly be dragged into "hands-on" activities and decisions. This is one of the reasons why you are so heavily overworked. Being overworked you will have little opportunity to manage the client. So the client will have *little opportunity to participate in the project as it proceeds*. Add this to *your lack of clarity about the project goals* and the *difficulties of catching up once* *things go wrong and you can see that it is **almost inevitable that your outcome stakeholders' needs will not be met**.'*

I sit there speechless. I feel a muscle tremor run down the back of my neck leaving a tingling sensation as if the hairs are rising. I know he is right.

'I always thought that learning was about something which happened in school, but I guess that I must be unrealistic if I think that I can handle projects, projects which are **always** something new, without learning all that there is to know about them **both** before and during them. And learning not just from being there but also from other people's experiences and knowledge. I need to relearn how to learn.'

Franck grins at me and I smile back. He says, 'One down,' and then noticing that the sun is starting to set, 'quick, there are no lights on the boat, we must get back before it gets dark.'

Chapter 6

BUBBLE No 2
RECOGNISING STAKEHOLDERS

It is hot and what is making me feel even hotter is the sight of Emily, Franck's daughter moving backwards and forwards along the beach. She started this a while ago and now the pace is faster. An hour and a half ago the tide had been out and it seemed a natural challenge for a nine year old, to build a sea wall of sand to keep the sea out. Armed with a long handled spade, she had quickly dug a trench along the beach six inches wide. The sand it had produced had been neatly stacked up as a formidable sea wall. The wall rises majestically upward a full four inches high. Encouraged by early success, the wall had grown in length and now extended seven metres in both directions, a magnificent sight. It was decorated, in parts, with sea shells and round pebbles. It is amazing what hard work and a readily mouldable material can produce.

The reason that she is running, East to West and then back East, is that, with the incoming tide, the sea is constantly trying to breach her defences. The main problem is that each wave attacks a different part of the buttress. Emily is continually trying to carry out repairs on the structure. The repair sites, however, keep shifting.

I look up at the sound of a Kawasaki sea scooter being ridden near the shore. The sound is loud, perhaps louder than normal, because Franck, who is lying on his side with his head on the picnic basket, stirs. He sits up and rubs his eyes, 'Bloody marvellous.'

'Fantastic,' I agree, 'did you have a good sleep then?'

'Yes. I did. Sorry, but I think I nodded off in the middle of you telling me something very interesting.'

I think to myself, 'But not interesting enough,' but instead I say, 'That's alright. It's too hot to think, let alone discuss anything serious.' I had been expounding my latest theory on why change is so difficult to manage.

I'm sitting next to a rock pool. As I'm trying to think of something to say next I notice that the surface of the pool is perfectly still, like a polished mirror. I reach across, pick up a pebble and I idly drop it in the water. I watch as the ripples move outwards from where the pebble was and reach the surrounding rock and then bounce back in together. As the ripples meet each other, the simple circular symmetrical pattern is broken and it becomes a furrowed undulating surface. It looks regular, more like a miniature, moving mountain range. I smile. So simple and yet so perfect. The energy from the falling pebble is systematically and gently dispersed in the water.

Franck leans over to see what I am up to. The surface is calm now. To demonstrate what I did before, I drop another pebble into the middle of the pond. The ripples spread slowly and symmetrically. I hear his voice over my shoulder say '**One Change Leads To Another**. Franck's First Law of Change.'

'Oh. So you're building a theory then?'

He says nothing, just smiles back.

I challenge, 'So what's Franck's Second Law then?'

In typical Franck fashion, he still says nothing, but reaches past me and grabs a handful of pebbles. He fixes me with his eagle eye stare and demands, 'Guess!' First he drops a single pebble into the pond. Then he flings half the handful of pebbles into the pond. There are several loud splashes. Drops of sea water rise into the air and fall back in causing further ripples. He waits about a second and then throws in half of what he has left and then a second later he chucks in the remaining pebbles. His demonstration started with a symmetrical pattern but after the first pebble the surface of the water has been a confused boiling. There has been no pattern at all. No clear ripples. There are even air bubbles and patches of foam on the surface. With his third throw a crab that had been sheltering under a small rock decides it is all too much and darts across the pond to take refuge under a larger rock.

'Well?'

I shrug, 'More pebbles make a bigger splash?'

'Not bad but not right.'

I venture cautiously, 'Don't throw all your pebbles in at once?'

'Definitely no! What did you actually observe?'

'You threw your pebbles in four lots'

'No. In the pond. Can you describe the pattern of ripples?'

'There was no pattern!' I exclaim. 'How could I possibly describe it?'

'Precisely! Congratulations you've worked out Franck's second law!'

'Huh?'

'If one change leads to another and a lot of changes are happening together it becomes increasingly difficult to predict what will happen next. **Adding change to change creates chaos.**'

I recognise this instantly. In my last two years at Infotech Solutions the directors had kicked off a large number of initiatives. Initiatives on quality, cost reduction, customer focus, efficiency skills development, competences, benchmarking and many others too numerous to list. Each initiative impacted on the others. Usually one initiative would change the goal posts of another. Sometimes they would compete for resources or management time. You never knew where the next thunderbolt would come from. One week we contacted one of our major customers six times! Six independent 'phone callers none of whom knew that the others were making calls, including two aggressive calls and one who slammed the 'phone down on the customer. In the end we had to give away a $50,000 piece of equipment to pacify him. An expensive surprise.

I nod slowly, 'Yes, you're right. Running a project in an organisation which is undergoing a lot of change, is a real bummer. Hey, this is good.'

Emily is standing still. She seems to be looking at two boys. The boys look roughly the same age as she is. It seems that in her enthusiasm to develop the wall she has extended it too far. She has encroached on their patch. True, their patch is badly defined, Mum and Dad lying in the shade of a pink beach umbrella a few metres from the shore. Picnic gear strewn haphazardly in the space between, a dismal looking sand castle or is it just a pile of sand, and a one foot deep crater dug out by hand. Watching them at a distance, barely being able to hear what is being said, is fascinating. I remember my own childhood. As I think of myself as a nine year old boy I can guess exactly what is going on and what is being said even though I can only hear some of what is being said. They seem unhappy about a girl who is doing something that they themselves had not thought of doing. You can tell that each boy wishes that he had thought of it first. You can tell from the nervous movements, shifting their weight from one leg to another that, now they have gotten used to the idea, it looks good fun. You can tell that they would love to join in but can't because it is a girl's idea and must therefore be a 'girlie' thing to do. Furthermore they don't like the idea of her building her wall on their patch even if it is a good idea. Emily backs down. After all, she has got enough work to do maintaining the existing wall. The extension seemed the right thing to do to make the wall complete. But it wasn't worth arguing over.

'What an amazing coincidence, the third law in practice.'

'Where?' I ask.

'There.' He points at the two boys who are still standing in the same place watching Emily return to work.

'What? You mean Emily trying to complete her wall, being prevented by two boys who are being territorial and anyway wish that they had thought up the idea first and won't play because they didn't.'

'Precisely! You really are getting good at working these laws out.'

I warm to the compliment and then realise I am not actually sure that I have really worked out the law. I clear my throat and ask 'How, er, do you phrase the law formally? I mean I can't really say to people, "Beware of little boys who won't let little girls play on their patch or play with them because the game wasn't their idea" can I?'

Franck tilts his head back and lets out a guffaw '**People Create Change – People Constrain Change**.'

Of course put that way it was so obvious, why hadn't I spotted it before? I had constantly done both. Suggestions and schemes put forward in meetings would get a thumbs down even if it was obvious that they were the right way to go. Three months later they were brought back out into the sunlight blinking but by now it was the group's idea or the idea of the only person who had opposed it most strongly. Of course – the age old trick of getting your boss to go along with something you want to do by trying to get the boss to think that it was his idea.

'Do you have any more laws that you could tell me?'

Franck replies cryptically, 'Yes and no.'

'Why not?'

'Because you can observe a lot just by watching.'

I follow his gaze. He is looking away from the rock pool and out towards the sea. Out at sea there are a few people swimming, one couple playing water polo. The chap on the sea scooter has just fallen off and is trying to re-mount his machine. Is that it? 'Change makes you fall off your perch?' I don't think so, it doesn't seem profound enough. I look further out, a few boats, one with a sail. In the foreground Emily is darting backwards and forwards more hurriedly than she had been earlier. I look back at the sail boat. The wind is blowing along the coast and they are having to tack to it. In order to keep parallel with the coast, they must be travelling in a zig zag fashion. 'That's it,' I think and I say out loud, 'Go with the flow.'

'What?' It's Franck's turn to be confused.

'The sailing boat. Go with the flow.'

'How can you read its name at this distance?'

I laugh, 'Now I come to think of it, with a project, success means changing things, you can't succeed if you go with the flow. Going with the flow means *you* change nothing. I give up.'

'Watch Emily,' he instructs.

By now she is darting backwards and forwards along her sea bank, even more furiously than before, mending the breaches in the wall, which each successive wave brought. No sooner has she finished rebuilding one section, then another section ten feet away is washed away. As the tide rises higher, the damage caused by each successive wave grows worse. There is more repair work to be done. Furthermore, with the long, twenty foot stretch of the wall, there is a good chance that up to three waves will strike along its length simultaneously. This is why, what had started out as a leisurely, fun activity, has changed into a frantic race against tide.

'Tell me what is happening.' he demands. 'What two facts of reality are interplaying?'

I think for a while and then say, 'The wall is too long.'

'Yes, in this world you avoid large single changes, *problems are diverse and inexhaustible, the opportunities for change are infinite.*'

'Emily can only work on one bit at a time.'

'Yes, *an individual's ability is bounded and has an end, there is certainly a limit to what you can do.* And what is the effect of the interplay of these two facts of reality?'

As I struggle to come up with an answer, I look across at her and see that Emily's growing tired and now after each repair she looks both right and left to assess both how far away the damage is and how bad it is. She does this to give her the best chance of maximum repair with minimum distance travelled.

My mind is letting me down. As I try to work out the answer to Franck's question, all that comes up is a series of proverbs; 'A stitch in time saves nine', 'Better to be hung as a sheep than as a lamb', 'Nothing ventured nothing gained'. And then it starts to cough up strap lines from advertisements '. . . reaches the parts other beers can't', 'Just do it'. I'm starting to feel a failure when I notice that Emily has abandoned the bulk of the wall and is simply concentrating on a small section. The section that was most heavily adorned with shells and pebbles. In fact she is having great success at reinforcing and building up that section. The section is now eight inches high and horse shoe shaped. But the best bit of all is that she is smiling and laughing now.

The sight of Emily gives me inspiration. I venture, 'Is it something about defining the boundaries of change which will allow you to succeed?'

'Very good. *If you try to range over infinite change and problems with limited resources and ability, your judgement will be biased and your spirit will end up exhausted.* Definitely, **Accomplished Change is Change Chosen and Carried out Carefully**.'

Franck has done it again. Starting off a project which is too ambitious or not ambitious enough, generally leads to the same thing, dissatisfaction. I can see his point but by now I know how Franck works, he never says anything these days without a reason. I ask, 'Why are you telling me this, I can't see what it has to do with my problem with projects.' He reaches across to the picnic basket and pulls out a napkin. I recognise it instantly. By now it is becoming an old friend. Creased and crumpled it looks like an old wise man who has seen all that the world has to offer. He smoothes it out with his left hand.

'Let's see . . . we never found out the underlying causes for this one.' His index finger is pointing at the bubble which said *lost business/unhappy sponsor*.

'Well, one reason is that the end users complain bitterly, to either the client or sponsor, about the delivered project. Another is that the sponsor and client react badly to surprises which you give them.'

'One at a time please. Remember the method we used before? Why don't you start with the first one, your reason to do with the end user.'

'The end users start to complain as soon as they discover that some of the output of the project is not to make their lives easier, if anything it makes them even more hassled.'

'What? You do projects which make the business worse?'

'Well I don't. Not really. In a few cases the project outcome is actually worse than the conditions preceding the project. Usually the real problem is that the users expect much more than they receive.'

'A mis-match between expectations?'

'That's right. Often you can deliver something which is more than adequate for the business needs but if the users have somehow got the idea that it is going to sing, dance and make pizzas, it will not be seen as success. If the client or sponsor hears the complaints, their view of project success becomes tainted.'

'What was your second reason?'

'Well I think that I've described an aspect of it. The client and sponsor tend to be really touchy. They tend to be easily upset if they discover something that they didn't know about in advance. They . . .'

Franck looks at his watch and then slaps his palm to his forehead and says, 'Shit a brick! There has been a change of plans, I have to get back to my *mas* by five. I'm afraid that I won't be able to give you a lift back to your apartment. Sorry I arranged it this morning. I . . .'

I'm pretty fed up. Franck's holiday *mas* is about twelve miles inland close to the village of *La Garde Freinet*. I know that it will take him about half an hour to get back and it's four thirty. He will have to leave at once, if he is to make his appointment. 'You could have said earlier, then we could have fetched my hire car,' I splutter.

Franck is smiling at me as if he has a private joke. It doesn't feel funny to me though. Visions of me taking an expensive taxi ride are passing through my mind and I'm starting to worry if I have enough cash to pay for it. I could have cashed a traveller's cheque in the town, if I had known earlier. The more worried I look, the broader his smile gets. Finally, I demand, 'What's so funny?'

'Don't be so touchy, you get upset so easily.'

He is quoting what I said earlier, back to me. Now he is giggling uncontrollably. 'You should see your face!' he says pointing at me.

It slowly dawns on me that I am having my leg pulled. 'Nice one, but couldn't you just have told me that no one likes surprises and that it is *my* fault and *not theirs*?'

'I don't think that it would have had the same impact somehow.'

'Well, this is the last time I accept a lift from you and become completely dependent on you!'

'I suspect that that is exactly how your stakeholders feel about you. That's how they feel if you fail to keep them up to date.'

'OK, OK, you win.'

'No. I don't. I don't win. Not until you tell me why the end-users become disappointed and why your other stakeholders find themselves surprised.'

I think for a second and then remember that we have already agreed that I tend not to manage the client, mainly this is because I am usually overworked. I remind Franck of our previous conversation. He agrees but asks, 'Is there anything else?'

I pause for a while and then say, 'Well, to be honest I hadn't really understood what managing the stakeholders is about. I thought that you were making a fuss over the idea of stakeholders and that it was all a bit academic. I now realise that since people constrain and create change, stakeholders are actually the source of *both* the hard success criteria and the soft ones. The need to meet certain financial targets or timeliness or a specific business outcome is driven by the vision of someone, some stakeholder.'

'And?'

'Since one change leads to another, the conditions in a project are bound to change from day to day. I need to be *capable of matching their expectations to what I am doing throughout the project*, **every day, on a day-to-day basis.** I have tended to assume that as long as they knew at the beginning what was supposed to be happening I didn't really need to influence their views during the project. In some cases I have actively avoided telling them anything at all.'

Franck nods. 'You will have unhappy stakeholders if you don't keep them up to date during the project and make sure reality matches their expectations. It's just like balancing stones on scales, you don't need to know the individual weights of the stones on either side, **just get them even that's all**.'

As I think about what Franck has just said, an image starts to form in my mind, a terrifying image, an image of me seated at an untidy desk. The in-tray of the desk is overflowing with paper and there are three 'phones on the desk. I have my elbows on the desk and I am talking into two of the phones at once. I am making 'phone calls to everyone in the company and writing endless memos explaining how late everything is getting, and it's getting later because I don't have time to do anything except keep everyone in balance.

'Great theory! But how can I manage everyone in the organisation at once?'

Franck doesn't seem to have heard me. He is intently watching Emily. Her sea wall has been converted into a sand castle. The castle is almost three feet high and has ramparts and turrets (all bucket shaped). Although the castle structure is much more grand than the sea wall was and contains much more sand, Emily doesn't seem to be rushing about as much as she had been earlier.

She spends some time working on the castle itself and then collects a bucket of sand and dumps it at the base and smoothes it out. The sea level has risen quite a bit and the waves are lapping at the base washing away the sand but she is actually depositing the sand **before** it needs repair. I suppose that makes sense; if she waited until there was significant damage by the more vigorous waves at the base, the sidewall of the castle would also collapse and she would have to repair not only the base but the side of the castle as well. She goes back to work on the castle itself for a few seconds and then notices that the sand around one of the sides has been worn away by the **last** wave so she stops to fix it. Watching her I notice that she has also dug two moat-like channels up each side. But instead of simply making the moat run around the castle she has used the channels to **divert** the flow of waves up the beach where the water can soak away gently without doing any damage to the castle. As we watch Franck asks, 'Do you see a pattern?'

I start to describe what she is doing. 'Work on castle . . . Reinforce base . . . Work on castle . . . Check for repairs . . . Work on castle . . . Reinforce base . . . Work on castle . . . Clear channels to divert waves . . . Work on castle . . . Reinforce base . . . Work on castle. Clever girl, she seems to have herself well organised.'

'Is that all?'

'And the castle is growing more and more splendid,' I add. 'Anyway you're just trying to dodge my question. I asked you earlier, how can I possibly manage everyone in the organisation at once?'

'What was the fourth law of change?'

I try to remember, 'Was it "**Accomplished Change is Change Chosen and Carried out Carefully**"?'

Franck nods slowly, as if he is hearing this law for the first time and is himself trying to make sense of it.

'What does that have to do with managing everyone in the organisation? It's a great idea but totally impractical. When I'm running a project all I need to do is to receive my briefing and I'm away. Being able to run with whatever you're given is the mark of an effective proj . . .'

'Who provides the brief?'

'The sponsor or client.'

'Don't you think any one else should be consulted or involved when you are formulating your brief?'

'No. The sponsor or client owns the project so it should be up to them to decide what the brief should be and how . . .'

'Number two!'

I stare. I'm starting to get irritated at being constantly interrupted. Franck is holding up two fingers. He twists his wrist to make a victory sign.

'If you do not identify all the stakeholders up front and use them to help you define what *they* think the brief is, let them define what is to be delivered and how it is to be done and hence be in a position to understand resource needs and their contribution and rewards from the project, it is almost impossible to balance their expectations and your outputs later.'

'Slow down.' I plead.

'In choosing your change carefully, you must spend time working out who the stakeholders are. They define for you the boundaries and organisation of your chunk of change. Watch.' Franck reaches into the picnic basket and pulls out a straw then he leans past me and floats it across the closest corner of the pool. It comes to rest against two rocks but forming a rough triangle. He then scoops up a handful of pebbles in his left hand and a single pebble in his right hand. As before he starts to throw the pebbles into the pool. He aims at the main part of the pool, not the sectioned off part. As before the surface of the main pool becomes choppy and frothy. The surface of the part of the pool cut off by the straw remains motionless. Franck then slowly raises his right hand and with a flourish of ceremony, drops a single pebble onto its calm surface. In contrast to the main pool, a regular ring of ripples forms and runs outwards.

I begin to understand. *'My stakeholders give me the best chance of succeeding, inspite of all four laws.'* My stakeholders determine *my* sectioned off part of the whole pool. *If I fail to **identify my stakeholders** at the **start** and make sure that they stay in place **throughout** the project I cannot guarantee success since outside change can easily enter my part of the pool and produce unpredictable results.*

I'm beginning to roll now, the ideas coming thick and fast. I remember Emily's wall. She could make little progress until she carefully chose the boundaries around the change which she wanted to carry out. 'You need to know all your stakeholders at the start, to get an understanding of the nature and size of your chunk of change.' I continue to use Emily's construction work as an analogy to help me think. I remember Franck instructing me to work out the pattern she used for protecting and developing the castle. And then it comes to me. *'And I don't have to*

51

worry about all of them all the time. Some are key in that they *define* and *support* the overall chunk of change; if you lose their attention or agreement to what you are trying to change, they have a tremendous impact on your progress. You find that you must spend even more time repairing the ill effects. It is best to protect them from any fallout. To balance them you must get to them **before** there is any trouble. Others you can handle as you go along, as long as you are alert and attentive. You can spot any problems they have from the **last** thing you or someone else did to them, and fix them. Some you simply want to **divert** away from your chunk of change because for them your project is a threat to their status-quo. They will "*drive a stake through it if they can*".' I am quoting from our first conversation and remembering why we called them stakeholders in the first place. I'm feeling quite pleased with myself. It is all starting to make sense.

Franck is nodding in agreement and adds, 'You use your stakeholders to help you to learn why the project is to be done and then separately to understand the idea behind it, the project concept.' I think I am following him as he continues, 'Imagine someone who doesn't understand stakeholder balancing. At the start they will fail to recognise important stakeholders, such as the boss of a particular specialist whose skills you need. They may approach the specialist and in so doing inadvertently offend the boss. The boss may then put barriers in the way of the specialist contributing to her project. If this happens, then usually an inappropriate team will be formed. It is difficult for an inappropriate team to work without making lots of mistakes or doing the wrong things which then have to be redone. It becomes *almost impossible* for the project to deliver the *specific technical and business objectives it was set up for.*'

I can't argue. It's spot on, but he continues. 'Imagine someone who doesn't understand stakeholder balancing. At the start they will fail to recognise the sponsor, or other senior managers or the board who have a stake. If they fail to gain senior management commitment at the start, they will find it difficult to get hold of resources. If there is little senior managers' commitment, prospective team members will not think that there are many "brownie points" to be obtained from working on the project. If this happens then it is difficult to get the best people in the organisation to become involved in the project, making the team inappropriate. If there is under-resourcing then, not only will it make it worse for the inappropriate team, they will constantly find themselves battling with all the odds stacked against them. What is even worse is that in addition other stakeholders such as the finance people will start to attack the project as it attempts to use resources which it has not been allocated. The direct impact of this will be to *make it difficult to achieve* the *financial contribution* of the project or meet its *timeliness in providing competitive advantage* and will almost certainly *demotivate the project team.'*

Franck has really got me thinking now. 'I guess that this is why it is such a big mistake to allow myself to become overworked. Any one who is overworked *and* doesn't really understand the concept of balance, stands little chance of managing their stakeholders effectively.'

'I agree, but look at the underlying problems,' he says, pointing at the napkin. I look down.

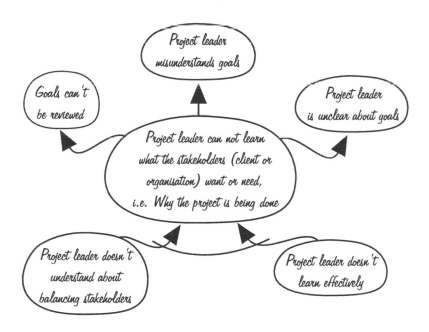

'The real killer happens for people who **neither** understand *stakeholder balancing* **nor** know how to *learn*. This combination makes it virtually impossible to *fully understand what the organisation needs and wants*. As a result the project leader *misinterprets* **both** the *goals* **and** the *means* of the project. The project fails from start to finish.

I'm sitting dumb struck at how it is all beginning to fit together. I have that sensation, you know the one which you have when you are shown one of those 'trick' pictures? The ones with two images superimposed into one. You get shown a picture of the ugly old lady, but if you try to imagine that her nose is a chin you suddenly see a beautiful young lady instead. For a split second, the power of the revelation is awesome. I look at Franck. He seems relaxed and content then we hear Emily. 'Finished! Finished!' She is shouting triumphantly. She is calling us over to look at her sand castle. We get up and walk towards her. It is a fantastic castle, a real achievement and she is standing proudly beside it beaming.

Chapter 7

SO SIMILAR AND YET
SO DIFFERENT

I wake up. The sun is streaming in through the window and it is deliciously hot. Hot enough to have started the cicadas singing. A day long opera, which will work up to a crescendo as the temperature rises further. I feel great. It really is wonderful to be on holiday. And in such great weather. And I have another two days. Two days? Only two days! As the sleepiness exits my brain it dawns on me that in two days I shall be back home and unemployed. I'd forgotten about that. I had been feeling quite good about my life until I remembered. I only have one possible opening and that was going to be a tough one to get through. I had eventually, after wasting another 260 francs, been able to speak to the senior partner of the Change Consultancy. I had liked the sound of her voice over the 'phone. It was in stark contrast to the difficulty that I had had in trying to talk to her, being bounced from one person to another in a formal and disorganised way. It was direct, warm and friendly.

She had introduced herself. Her name was Cathy Stork. She had been brief and to the point. She had said that in the modern business environment what organisations were looking for was consultants who were not normal consultants. Consultants who really understood what the client was going through and had ideas which could help. They wanted someone who would help them implement these ideas. What her partnership was therefore looking for was an additional partner, to help to cope with this growing demand. The one and only yardstick which would be used to choose this person was, 'Does this person know more about managing change than we do and do they understand it well enough to help the other partners learn?' Everything else from past track record to personality was far less important to them because they felt that anyone who understood change better than they did and was willing to help them learn more would share many beliefs and values and would probably fit right into the organisation. Currently they were all bound together by a burning desire to further understand change better and to make lots of money out of it.

Cathy had asked me how it sounded. I had said that it sounded fine. Then she had told me that they would be happy to meet with me for an interview but only if I felt that I had something new to offer, otherwise they would save us all time by suggesting that I looked elsewhere. She had asked me how that sounded. I had replied that I would very much look forward to meeting them on my return. I had my fingers crossed behind my back as I told this lie. I wasn't sure that I really had anything new to offer about change but I thought 'Who knows? There is almost another week to go, until an interview. Maybe, somehow, by some amazing miracle, by some freak of nature or a rupture in the space-time continuum, by the time the interview comes round I will be the fount of all knowledge.'

I throw back the thin sheet, get out of bed and head for the bathroom. I guess my life is like many other people's. I am usually centre stage. I spend time trying to work out what to do next. It goes in phases. My idea of what I want to do with my life keeps changing. Sometimes the phases are distinct, sometimes they run into one another. When I was a teenager I knew precisely *what* I wanted to do. I wanted to be a world famous scientist. I knew exactly what to do but *not how*. It was a great feeling; really exciting. I felt just like a knight *going* off *on* some marvellous **quest**. I felt as if I had my own personal Holy Grail which I was seeking and I could overcome any obstacles to get to it. My options were **semi-closed**. It's true that no one ever actually found the Holy Grail but I remember reading in Steinbeck's novel that Arthur actually never expected the Grail to be found. He was just trying to provide a purpose for his Knights of the Round Table, to give them something to do to stave off the boredom once the kingdom was at peace. The purpose of the Grail was not to be found . . . but to be sought. And sought in as many ways and places as possible.

When I graduated I had all the skills I needed. I knew *how* to do all the things expected of a graduate scientist, but I had little idea of *what* I wanted to do with them. In the end I simply ended up taking the first offer I was made. I remember feeling a bit disappointed, capable of anything in the right field but without a clear aim. It reminded me of my 18th birthday. I got a marvellous present. I got a movie camera. What an opportunity. In a short time I had figured out how it worked, how to load it, how to focus. It was great. But somehow after the first rush of excitement it ended up spending a lot of time in the bottom drawer of my chest of drawers. I'd often come across it and feel excited, but the real problem was that, although I knew how to use it I didn't have anything to use it for. On my birthday itself and on the few days which followed I had made a few 'shorts'. You know the sort of thing; brother in the garden, cat climbing onto shed, me wriggling my toes whilst singing in a nasal tone. Without really knowing what to do, I would often suggest to my friends 'Let's *make a **movie***'. We would then spend an hour arguing over what the movie was going to be about. It seemed as if our choices were **semi-open**. If we agreed, we would develop something mediocre if we didn't we would find our day gone without doing anything else. So, the camera spent a lot of time in my bottom drawer.

There have also been times in my life when I have known both. I have known what to do and how to do it. These have been some of the most tiring periods of my life. I have found myself working hard to realise a dream which was so solid and **closed** that all it needed was work to make it come true. At such times I have usually got a pretty clear idea of what was to be done step-by-step. All I had to do is work to fill each step in. It is almost like '***painting by numbers***'. Each shape clearly outlined, each shape numbered to tell you which colour to use, all you have to do is select whether to use the thick or thin brush.

And then there was now. I am neither sure of exactly what I want to do next nor how I am going to do it. All my options seem **open**. Everything seems possible but I can't really see where I am going. It's a bit like trying to make your way in a ***fog***. The only way that I can make any progress is to decide for a short time which option to pursue, pursue it and then stop and take stock of how it's going and whether I think that it is worth pursuing further.

'Funny old thing that. Life certainly is all change.' I'm sure that I've heard someone say that recently. I screw my eyes up as I try to remember who it was. I begin to think that it might be the words of a song but then I remember, '*For most people, life is all change.*' Franck had said that when we were on the island. I wonder if my descriptions of my life will apply to the projects which I have been involved in. I reach for the toothbrush and start to apply pressure to the tube of paste. It's hard work squeezing out a line of blue and white gel. Hard work for my fingers because the tube has taken about all the squeezing that it is going to. Early in its life, I squeezed it in the middle a lot. A habit which I have had since I was a teenager. It always used to bug Sam. My eyes narrow and moisten. Thinking of Sam makes me feel lonely for a second. But I can't help it. It's a habit that I can't give up because I never notice myself doing it. My squeezing has created a constriction, which means that, although I have used up about half of the paste available, I have come to the end of the useful life of the tube.

'Funny.' I think. 'I was taught to think about projects mechanically, as something with a beginning – a middle and – an end. Now I'm not sure. Maybe they are more complex than that? Maybe they are more fluid than that? Maybe the way a project turns out depends on whether you squeeze it in the middle?' I smile to myself. I notice my reflection in the mirror and instinctively hold in and then pat my stomach. A futile gesture which reminds me of the effect, of the five-fish, variety bouillabaisse dish I consumed last night. I feel guilty, about eating non-stop but as usual I simply remind myself that I am supposed to be on holiday. I protest out loud, 'This is France. You're supposed to pig out.' And there is nothing like freshly baked croissants, washed down with freshly squeezed orange juice and a cup of steaming strong freshly brewed coffee for breakfast to help one feel fully content and yet awake and full of life and I know just where to find such a marvellous breakfast.

I sit on the edge of the bed and put on my left sandal. I try to think a bit more of projects which will fit into the categories which I have been playing with. Franck had said that the only way to manage change was in chunks. He'd also said that it was a different thing to work out why you needed to implement the change from working out the ideas behind the change. What was it he had called it? The germ of an idea. The *project concept*. I try to decide whether my idea about projects relates to the reasons for carrying out the project or whether it relates to the ideas behind the project. I'm not sure. I decide to focus on the ideas behind the project rather than focus on why it is taking place. That feels right to me.

I have a five minute walk down to the restaurant on the sea front where I know I can get a great breakfast. It would probably be a minute if I could get there directly but I have to go around the houses and there is a fast dual carriageway to cross. I set off whistling. I really do love sunshine. 'Hmm,' I say out loud, 'A project where we know what to change to and how to make the change happen?' The building site project, the one with all the brick layers and architects and surveyors was definitively painting by numbers. I agree that it's a pretty complex painting. But it certainly had each group painting in their own colour into their well defined area. As long as they painted up to the lines carefully and didn't overlap too much or leave empty white spaces the masterpiece selected by the architect would be reproduced.

I like the idea. The project is closed because the original masterpiece defines what the picture should look like and how the colours should be filled in. I guess that it is easier to apply this to a Toulouse Lautrec poster than to Monet's impressionist paintings of poplars. Lautrec's use of relatively few bold colours and shapes would require some work to draw out the shapes. The Monet would need more. There'd be a lot more work to do in defining the blank painting, since the same colour is repeated in small patches in order to create the impressionist image. I reckon you could easily get fed up with painting the Monet. Because the same colours are used in smaller patches more often and it all has to come together to give you a finished painting. If you weren't co-ordinated you would spend all your time washing out and changing brushes.

The reason that closed projects are difficult to manage is because they *require many distinct skills which must be interwoven to produce the desired result.* **Breaking down** *the overall job into specific activities and* **co-ordinating** *them as they are carried out, is very difficult. What we try to do each time with closed projects is to make the copy more and more like the original, faster, cheaper. This is very challenging.*

I stop and wait for a gap in the traffic so that I can run dangerously across the road. It's a busy morning and the traffic continues in a steady stream for a while. I start to daydream as I wait. 'Hey! This is working, are there any others?' It hits me. 'Of course that was why our *Locos* ran and ran.' They were quests. Our programmers kept trying ever more sophisticated methods to try to deliver the ultimate solution to the client! That was why they were constantly 90 per cent of the way there. They were, but each time it was on a different methodology.

The reason that semi-closed projects are so difficult to manage is because **what** *the project is set to achieve is* **clear** *and* **compelling** *and* **seductive**. *It's usually a big sexy idea. We feel, 'If only we could get there it would all be wonderful'. People are prepared to try,* **forever**, *different routes of getting there.*

I chortle, this is almost too easy. 'OK. What about a movie? Find me a movie.' I try to think. A project based around a method, searching for an objective. 'Ha! My mad professor.' He spent all his time working on different applications for the equipment he'd invented. If that isn't a movie then I don't know what is. That was why our goals kept moving. It was because he knew how he was going to do the research but not what it was really going to contribute and anyway his interest was in using the equipment not in achieving the goal of meat substitutes!

The reason that semi-open projects are difficult to manage is because *the project concept is **based on** a certain **methodology** or **resource** or **process** and may be owned by people who really enjoy using the methodology. What is to be achieved has less of a profile and may be **frequently changed***.

I'm starting to feel smug and then it hits me. A blinding dazzling light. Like when you are on an aeroplane which takes off on a dark wet overcast day and climbs steadily through dark heavy clouds and then suddenly bursts out from below them into the sunshine. I realise the reason I quit my job. I realise that it was not because **I** was wrong or because my directors were. I realise that the main barrier to us making progress with 'Go-For-It' was that although we were all too embarrassed to admit it, we were caught in a thick fog. Caught unaware, without a compass to refer to. The fog had come down whilst we were off the footpath, so we had no reference point at all. Striding off first in one direction and then in another. Going rapidly round in circles. No! Worse than going round in circles, going around in a random fashion, like a headless chicken. And because no one would admit to the fog we all individually knew that we were lost in, we continued to strut pur-posefully rather than continually take stock and make slow steady progress in one direction. One step at a time. 'How dumb! If only we had known better. The problem is, that in our organisation we were expected to know all the answers. All our management activities, meetings, milestones, measurements, budgets assumed that you were painting by numbers!'

The reason that open projects are so difficult to manage is that *however hard you try your **ideas never** become **clear**. So you must deliver benefits in spite of not knowing what the final outcomes will be. You must **focus** your attention on the best ideas of what is to be done and the best ideas of how to do it, **do it** and then **check** to see how progress is going and then repeat the steps. Delivering any benefits at all as opposed to drifting aimlessly is critically dependent on your ability to constantly **do, review, learn** from what you have done, **replan** and **repeat** the cycle again. **Do, review, learn plan and do***.

I'm feeling good now as I walk into the restaurant. It must be showing on my face because as I walk in everyone I meet smiles broadly at me and says '*Bonjour*'. I reply using my best French pronunciation and smiling back but really all I want is to be shown to my table as quickly as possible, so that I can get reimmersed into my thoughts. I am shown to a table between a window and the door to the kitchen. I waste no time. 'Is this right?' I think, 'have I really just invented a method of explaining to myself how the idea behind a project determines how it is going to be difficult to implement and in which particular ways or areas the difficulty is going to arise? Or is it something everyone, except me, already knows? Am I teaching my grandmother to suck eggs?' I have always had this problem. Perhaps it's something to do with my teachers at school when I was a kid? Perhaps it's to do with me. But whenever I discover something with my own mind or from my gut feelings, I can't believe that it is right. I always feel that, since I thought of it, it can't be of any value or it's really obvious to every one else. I try hard to think whether I have ever read or heard anything about different types of projects anywhere. I can't. 'I wonder if this is new enough to discuss when I go to see Cathy about the job? I'll just have to try it out and see. Now it seems so obvious, five minutes ago it didn't.'

The coffee and warm croissants arrive. 'Mmm . . . What a heavenly smell!' The sensation is like the smell of the first drops of rain after a long drought. I drink it in for a second and then pounce. When I eat fresh croissants I don't add jam or butter. Adding to the perfect, makes imperfect. I bite on the left arm of the crab. The croissant melts in my mouth. I chew slowly. 'Delicious.' The full experience is not just the olfactory it is also the eating. 'It's not just the idea behind the project it is also the way you carry it out.' I giggle silently and take another bite, a larger one than the first, off the right arm. With some projects the progress you are making is obvious to everyone. You can tell how far you have got. It is easy to measure how well you are doing. Like my building project. In fact, it can sometimes be a real pain because everyone can tell if you are succeeding or failing.

With such a **visible** project keeping tabs on progress is easy, but you need to put some effort into making sure that everyone sees it in the same light. I smile to myself as I remember the time that the brick layers managed to brick up all the doors on the ground floor. There had been an error on one of the drawings and half of them were working to the first floor plan, whilst the others were working to the ground floor plan. I remember hearing shouts and some elaborate insults relating the supervisor's brain to a peanut, then a walnut and then a soggy sponge. Yes indeed, the cock-up was obvious. I'm sure that the supervisor wished it had been less visible. For weeks afterwards the brick layers were the continuous butt of all the jokes on the site. What was the childish one which always made me smile? I remember. 'What is the difference between a brick layer and a brick? One's only good for making walls and the other is only good for making walls!' I don't think they enjoyed that experience much. I look up and notice that the couple across the door are watching me bemused. My enjoyment must be obvious and I am making rapid progress round the croissant.

My culture change project was not like that at all. No one knew exactly what progress had been made. Not even me. The only really visible thing was the money which had been spent. How could we see if the culture was changing? We could see some of the visible tasks such as the training courses which we set up, but progress in the culture change itself was not obvious or measurable. Hey! That is just like our *Loco* projects. For those also it was hard to measure progress. Nor was it obvious. Not even the people who were actually working on the tasks, such as the programmers, could gauge how much progress they were making. It was almost impossible for anyone outside the immediate project team to have the slightest idea of how well we were doing. If you left it alone, the progress of the project could almost have been **invisible**. With this new insight I drop my head into the palms of my hands, squeeze my eyes shut tightly and rock my head rhythmically from side to side. That was why the other directors found it so easy to hijack parts of my culture change project and push forward their own pet projects. How dumb. If only I had devised ways of making progress more obvious and found ways of measuring it frequently it would have been far easier to manage the project without it going out of control. No wonder we lost control of the *Locos*. Anything would have helped. Even asking three people once a week what they thought about the culture and plotting it on a graph would have given me a measure of progress, however inaccurate. We should also have kept closer tabs on our *Locos*: found some way of making progress more measurable. I slurp my coffee.

I'm on my second croissant now. Surprisingly it tastes just as good as the first. I take another large swig of my hot coffee. This is really great, this sitting, this looking over the sea, watching the shadows shorten. This consuming marvellous pastry. I had had a short spell about three years ago where I had decided that it would be really great to bake my own bread. That way I could have freshly baked bread every morning. I had bought a bread maker, a Knetworld Master Baker Plus. It was a large, white, device which stood two feet high and looked a bit like a giant, coffee maker. It had four compartments on the top. One for flour, one for water, another for butter and a yeast pot. But you know how it is, when you have to measure up quantities and set up the equipment last thing at night before you turn in. It is very difficult to keep it up. Early on, I forgot to load up the equipment a few times. I could always make excuses for myself. It's easy, when you're your own customer, to let your quality and delivery standards drop.

The *progress of projects can be largely* **visible** *or* **invisible**. The level of visibility *depends on* the specific nature of *the project activities*. With a visible project progress is obvious to all the stakeholders and progress is easily measurable. The *stakeholders can* therefore *make up their own minds* about how well it's going. *To succeed you must* **manage what your stakeholders observe** *in order to ensure that they are kept in balance.*

Invisible projects can only be managed by *inventing additional progress indicators and paying a lot of attention to them*. Unless you do all you can to make progress obvious, people will either *forget* about you or will think that you are *failing* and you'll find it *difficult* to get the support that you need from your stakeholders.

So the idea behind the project influences how it should be managed but so do the actual activities which you need to co-ordinate. My thoughts are becoming well structured. I feel good, but I have a small nagging voice at the back of my mind as if I have forgotten something. I frown, trying hard to listen to it. I figure that it must be something to do with Franck. What would he say about the conclusions I've just reached? I can't think of anything which he could say to destabilise me. But I still feel uncomfortable. Nothing I have said violates his laws. '*One change leads to another; adding change to change causes chaos; people create change – people constrain change*'; and I'm even helping out on his fourth by classifying the types of project idea and the way in which its progress is happening. I am adhering to his '*Accomplished change is change chosen and carried out carefully.*'

The waiter comes up and asks if I want anything else. 'Another pot of coffee please,' I reply. He writes this on my bill and puts the bill on the table. I reach into my back pocket to get some cash out to pay. I've enjoyed the meal and feel generous I might even leave a tip. And then it hits me, paying for a service, of course! It makes a difference whether the stakeholders are paying for the project or not. People create change – people constrain change. People constrain change when someone else imposes it on them. *It makes a real difference who is to change as a result of the project.*

In a **commercial** project the change is undertaken by one group in order to provide the outcome for another group – the key stakeholders – who are outside the organisation which is managing the change. For the project leader the project is **external**. The project leader finds themselves bound by legal contracts and under great pressure to make some money out of the deal. In some ways this is easier, because people go out of their way to specify as clearly as they can, what is to be done and how it is to be done and usually to write it down. I guess it's the opposite if the project is **internal**. A *change* project, run inside your own organisation, does not work that way. There are no legally binding agreements. In fact, people feel quite free to 'mess you about', as much as they like. Also, there is no chance of making money out of the project itself. If any money is made, it is as a result of someone else exploiting the opportunities which the project has provided. I remember that other great watershed of my career, my office move project and then I realise; 'Internal projects are not simply the opposite of external projects.' It is not just that your key stakeholders and the people who are to change as a result of the project are in the same organisation as you. It's worse. Because *you* are part of the same office political system, making progress is like swimming in shark infested treacle.'

I finish my coffee and leave the money on the table. I walk to the door, 'Merci,' and out. The blinding sunlight hits me. I blink and put on my dark glasses. I walk round the corner feeling I'm pretty smart. I try to summarise what I have found out, so that I can remember it better. 'For every project there is an idea, some gain which you wish to hold onto. The ideas fall into four groups. The group it falls into has an overriding impact on what approach and skills are required to manage it. In order to effectively draw a decent boundary around your chunk you must manage stakeholders. If they are internal or external to you makes a great difference. And then to stand the best chances of control you must understand the natural visibility of the project activities.'

'There is a *tremendous difference* between trying to manage a *closed, external, visible* project and an *open, internal, invisible*, project. If the project is closed then we know what we are doing and how it is to be done so our stakeholders know what their roles are and it is easier to communicate what is to be done. We can set milestones and check points wide apart since we do not need to constantly monitor everything. Since it is external, many of our actions and our stakeholders' actions, will be set by contractual agreements and being visible it will be easy to monitor progress.'

'If the project is open then we will find it very difficult to clarify to ourselves what is to be done or how it is to be done. We will even have difficulty deciding who our stakeholders are. Because it is open we will find it difficult to communicate and almost impossible to clearly assign roles. In fact the roles may keep changing. Being internal, the politics will make it very difficult for us to make progress and we may find it difficult to get the degree of top level support we need (this is made worse by it being open. The top level may feel nervous about signing into something that they don't fully understand). Finally being invisible we will have to watch everything, all the time or else it will go out of control. Also we will find it very difficult to demonstrate that we are making progress and will constantly be under pressure to perform.'

I wait to cross the road again. That's not bad. I guess reality is a bit more complex than I've worked out but I decide to have another think, once I have got used to the ideas. I feel that I may find it easier and easier to spot the pitfalls of any combination of project characteristics well in advance, without having to have lived through one of that type. I wish I had understood the difference two years ago. It might have given me a better chance of success.

There is a spring in my step as I realise, 'Maybe I do have something to offer Cathy after all.'

Chapter 8

BUBBLE No 3
GAINING PERSPECTIVE

I'm lost. I've got a map so I shouldn't be. Perhaps I should've looked at it before setting off. I don't know where I am, so I can't find myself on the map. I'm fed up. These blasted hairpin bends. I suppose, for someone in a better mood, they're charming and the changing scenery is inspiring. But for me, it is not. I have started to curse Franck. I imitate him putting on a heavy, slurred, Australian accent. 'Come on mate. It'll be great if you come and spend your last night with us. You want to see the bush in this country. There's a fete on in the village we could go to and have a rave up. It's not so far and it's really easy to find and anyway since our holiday *mas* is further inland, it's on your way home.' Franck could always talk me into anything. His technique was to keep talking without appearing to breathe until I caved in. He said it was a technique which he learnt from playing the digeridoo, a sort of early Australian, Aborigine, saxophone.

I hate to admit it but I'm lost. I give in and decide to stop at the next habitable place I see and try out my broken French. Then my car comes round the corner and I see a sign saying, '*La Garde Freinet*'. I punch the air. 'Yo!' Now all I have to do is first find the village centre, then find and set off down the road on the right, past the boule court, four miles up into the hills and I should be there.

What Franck has neglected to tell me is that the four miles are up a single width dirt track, with a blind corner every two hundred yards. I inch my way up, concentrating on negotiating the bends. Not too fast, in case I lose control, not too slow, in case the plume of dust I have raised catches up with me. I do not really notice that I'm climbing. I continue for about fifteen minutes and then I reach a fork in the road. The left fork leads downwards and is signposted 'Le Bon Domicile'. The right hand fork leads upwards. The sign post for this fork is obviously home made. It has a black, black background. A white horseshoe in the top right hand corner represents a crested moon. In a wide band across the top but randomly spread are some white blobs, which I take to be stars. A thin, white streak ending in a blob, which I take to be a shooting star, runs in an arc along the top, from left to right. Along the bottom of the sign it reads '*Le Mas sous les Etoile*'. I try to translate. 'The . . . Farmhouse . . . on . . . the Stars? No! That can't be right. The Farmhouse under the Stars.' I'm pleased with myself.

I turn up the hill and straight into another of those bends. The car struggles up a steep slope bouncing along on the rubble, its wheels spinning and sending out a thicker pall of dust. I round the corner and there it is, the farmhouse. But the building does not keep my attention. I notice it. I notice the view. Imagine that you were sitting on one of the most beautiful beaches in the world, feeling content with the world and a helicopter had landed near you and offered to take you up. You had accepted and got in. The pilot had asked you to close your eyes and then had taken you about twelve miles inland and high. High enough so that when he asked you to open your eyes you could almost see horizon to horizon and out across the beautiful beach which you had been sitting on earlier. A breathtaking view, the sort for which you allow your mouth to fall open but don't care. And the excitement, the excitement of being so high up in the air your heart pounds at the prospect of falling, your brain buzzes at the new perspective that this world has to offer. But I am not in a helicopter. I am sitting in a hire car driving the last few yards to the top of the world. To my left is this mixed sensation. To my right is a small sharp pointy crag.

They are expecting me. I guess they could see me coming for miles, especially with that plume of dust. Franck hands me a can. 'This is absolutely incredible! It's bloody marvellous! How ever did you find this place?' Emily rushes up. I lift her up and give her a kiss.

'Friend of a friend,' he replies, as we walk towards the *mas*. Emily is dragging me by my left hand.

'Yes, I will race you underwater. Hello.' I kiss Rosabeth on the cheek. 'Great to see you again. Yes, we can dive for coins, same rules, who ever gets the coin keeps it and I supply all the coins. Rose, this is really something.' I look out over the brim. 'I feel as if I could see forever.'

'Perspective, use it or lose it,' says Franck. 'With perspective we have a sense of the current and the future stretching away ahead of us. We have a sense of what to do now in order to influence our future.'

I'm not really listening. Food is being put out on a long white plastic table on the veranda. It is attracting my attention. It looks and smells like the sort of meal which I usually have seconds and then thirds of. 'Mmmmm smells delicious. What is it?'

It has been a great lunch. Now Emily and Rosabeth are stretched out on the sun lounges, fast asleep. I start to tell Franck what I have discovered about the project concept, the stakeholder boundaries and it's visibility. It gushes out in an unsorted manner. Franck listens patiently whilst I unscramble it all and rearrange it all.

Finally he speaks. 'That really is brilliant. It helps explain some of the things which I have observed but not been able to explain.' I described the project concept as the germ of an idea behind the chunk, now you are describing it as a seed. 'Of course! If projects come as different types of seeds you would expect them to grow up to be different plants with different characteristics and fruits! It seems to me that from your analysis of how open a project is and whether the stakeholders are internal or external and whether it is visible or not, you should be able to work out in advance the types of problems which you will encounter.'

I think for a moment, I think I see what he means 'Oh you mean if it is open and invisible you will have a constant battle to explain what you are up to and to get people to sign on. Not only are you unsure of what to do or how to do it but you can't easily show someone what is required or what you have been doing.'

Franck nods. 'Needs more work to fully understand how you can use the characteristics of the project to help you to look into the future, to crystal ball gaze. Hang on, I'll get our fellow traveller to join us.' He disappears into the house and reappears a minute later waving the crumpled napkin. He is brandishing it like a flag.

'So? We often end up with fruits which we didn't want,' he says pointing to the bubbles at the top of the napkin. I smile. The overall effect of all his lines bubbles and arrows are a bit like a tree. Well, a short fat bush covered in ripe, fat, fruit. 'Anyway, tell me a bit more about these errors and redone tasks.'

'Well,' I start, 'we decided that we redid tasks because we had not met the client's requirements and because we made errors.'

'Yes.' Franck nods.

I continue. 'But it might also be that we are actually carrying out activities which are very hard to do and have a low chance of success.'

'How come?'

I proceed slowly. 'Well if in advance we didn't really understand how risky the activities were, we would undertake them without anticipating how hard they were going to be. We would not waste time finding out more about them and that would lead not only to errors but to us being a bit surprised by the things that went wrong. So we could end up having to redo tasks not because they were actually wrong but because we later discovered a better or less risky route.'

'So what you are saying is that if the project leader does not evaluate the risks of the project in advance this will almost certainly lead to the hard criteria of money, timeliness and purpose not being met?'

'I guess so.' I answer, nodding. It sounds clearer when Franck says it.

He assumes I'm with him and carries on. 'And it is even worse if you don't really know the point that the chunk has reached at any time. I mean which critical points have been passed and which critical points are coming up next.'

My back goes straight and I wince. I've had enough of these obvious but painful realisations. I'm beginning to think that spending time with Franck is not as much fun as I thought it was. 'Of course!' I realise. 'Unless you have *a very clear idea of the status of the project at all times* in the project, you may feel uncomfortable about allowing your outcome stakeholders to get too close to what you are doing. You feel vulnerable and uncomfortable in case 'they find you out' and so you *can't* really *keep your outcome stakeholders up to date*. Also there is no way that you *can keep your other stakeholders, such as your team or suppliers informed of progress* or really understand *who to put pressure on and when*!'

I explain this to Franck who simply nods and asks, 'If it is so important to know this thing you call "the status of your project" at all times then why is it that often in the past you haven't?'

I pause for a second. 'Well,' I confess looking sheepish, 'sometimes with smaller projects I kid myself into thinking that I can handle them without needing plans at all. It never works though, unless the project is really small and closed and even when that project works it often eats into my time for something else and messes that up instead.'

'Anything else?'

'Yes I think we talked about it a bit when we met in the restaurant. Some plans are a real bugger to update.'

'Oh?' Franck's eyebrows are almost touching his hairline.

'Well, if you have a computer generated time schedule, for example, you often need to dedicate a whole person to the task of keeping the schedule up to date. It's the same for the cash flows and monitoring milestones.'

'I'm sorry,' he says, 'I'm not sure that I actually understand what you mean by . . .'

I charge ahead across him speaking quickly, 'It's quite simple really. You see what you do is to work out all the tasks and activities you intend to carry out and then arrange them sequentially with their durations . . .'

'. . . planning?'

'What?' I ask.

'I was saying that I was not sure that I understood what you actually meant by planning. How would you explain the purpose and method of planning to a layman like me?' Franck says in his patient voice. I fail to notice that I am being set up and answer.

'Well, what you do is that you take the overall job and break it into its component parts. There are different forms of plan the most common is based on something called critical path analysis. You arrange all your tasks in a sequential order, doing things in parallel where possible and by estimating how long things take you can establish the precise sequence, which if late will make everything else late. You can also write this up as a sort of diary on a bar chart it is something called a Gantt chart. Also you can work out the cash flows against the activities and develop performance indices.'

'I see,' he says calmly, and then the killer, 'and this applies to **all** your forms of project: your walking in the fog, movie, quest and painting by numbers? What happens if you do not know the component parts of your project, if you do not know all the steps?'

'Erm.' I stall for time. I don't know the answer. 'Well, I have used this method a lot in the past for planning. I guess that it must apply to all of them equally.'

'Oh! Even the fog?'

'I suppose that that might be slightly different.' I am lying. I know for a fact that the method I described does **not** work for fog-like projects. I tried it on my corporate culture change project and it hadn't worked. For a start I couldn't break the job down since I didn't really know what it needed as component parts. What was even worse was that for the few things that I knew needed doing, I had no idea how long they would take. I had produced a critical path chart but it was so incomplete as to be total nonsense.

'You said that the plans were difficult to update. Does this mean that things do not happen as you plan for them to or does it mean that the planning method is too complex?'

'My problem is that I do not have enough data for developing the plan.'

Franck stares into my eyes and says with that steely voice I have heard before. 'No. That is not your problem. Your problem is that you do not know what planning is.'

'I do know what planning is,' I protest, raising my voice. On the sun lounge Rosabeth stirs slightly, turns over and goes back to sleep. 'I've done it enough times. As long as you have the right software its really straight forward.'

'If you know how to plan, then how come you end up with unusable plans which you cannot update. Your stakeholders don't know what's going to happen and what their stake in it is: especially for your team, how come it doesn't motivate them and how come you find it so necessary to stay close to the action and can't delegate?' He delivers this in a steady stream calmly. It goes through me like an ice dagger. Then the twist. 'An ideal person thinks of trouble and *prevents* it.'

I sit there stunned. I'm feeling a bit annoyed.

He ignores me and continues. 'You must choose the appropriate planning method to match the type of project. You may have selected inappropriate methods to *track your progress* and to *co-ordinate* your activities, which is why you find it difficult to *update your schedules*; that makes it difficult to *review your actual progress* and makes it difficult to *communicate* clearly the needs of the project to the right stakeholders, at the right time but you're *not* talking about planning. If you don't review then you won't change your plans. You won't check your goals or be able to catch up if you fall behind. Not reviewing your goals makes it very likely that you'll not deliver what is required by your client. If you understood the real nature of planning this would not happen.' He delivers this in the same manner as before looking straight at me with his quiet voice sounding like a deafening roar.

'Look,' I insist, 'I *do* know about planning. I've done it many times. I've even read books on the subject. Why are you giving me such a hard tim . . .?'

He talks over me. 'Success with your chunk is not just what you achieve as the success of one day or one stakeholder, nor is failure the failure of just one day or stakeholder. Both success and failure come from gradual development.'

'What are you talking about? I've run projects. I understand planning. I understand how to . . .' My voice trails off. Franck is not listening to me. Instead he's looking out over the marvellous view which we have in front of us.

Getting no response to my outburst I gaze out in the same direction. My mind is still in turmoil tinged with emotion. I think 'What does he mean?' 'What does he mean?' 'What does he mean "track my progress"?' My anger doesn't last. The view is too beautiful. I get caught up by the beauty of the scene and only faintly hear *'Perspective. Use it or lose it.'* 'Pardon? What did you say?' I question.

'Nothing.' 'Except number three.'

'Number three', meant that Franck felt that he'd found my third underlying cause of project failure. But what had he found? My curiosity overcomes my animosity and I ask, 'What have you found?'

'Any one who doesn't realise that *the true nature of planning is to* **continuously gain and maintain perspective** and that the *true nature of co-ordination and control is to* **spread and use the perspective amongst stakeholders**, and that the two things are two *separate* processes will find it difficult to consistently succeed with projects.'

My brain turns slowly. I'm trying to understand what I've just heard. I do this by putting it into my own words. 'You mean, what I need to do, is actually **two** different things. *I need to constantly seek out my objectives, and the* **constraints** *to achieving my objectives and how the different constraints interact* and that the rest of it is just about *finding ways of* **communicating** *this to stakeholders so that they also posses a similar perspective*?'

'I think that you put it better than I do,' he says with warm admiration.

I shake my head in a mixture of wonder, despair and elation. Gaining and maintaining perspective is how I understand what constrains all the stakeholders and therefore the project. It also helps me understand how the project activities constrain each other. I then need time schedules, cost schedules, responsibility matrices, etc. simply to communicate who depends on who or what and who is to do what and when: to find out what is not happening when and how I hoped it might and again communicating the changed demands on the stakeholders. To manage change successfully you must choose the methods best suited to that type of chunk. Mechanistic methods for closed projects. Fluid methods for open projects. Of course! And with perspective you understand that you don't have to manage everything all the time.

'You know you asked me about communication?'

My mind chases and I answer with a vague air, 'Yes.'

'Well it seems that we have found where it fits in,' he looks back at me and smiles.

I feel a fly tickling the back of my ear and instinctively swat at it. But it isn't a fly. It's a leaf and next to it is a cheeky face, attached by a neck, shoulder and arm to the hand which is moving the leaf back and forth. 'Can we dive for coins now? Please?'

I pull a face.

'Pleeeease?'

'OK.' And with that she dives head first into the pool and I head for the house to change.

Chapter 9

BUBBLE No 4
PEOPLE AND ME

We hear the music before we see the lights. It's hot and the car windows are open. '. . . *Docteur Jekyll et Monsiuer Hyde . . . Par hasard, pas rasé . . .*' The *boule* court is acting as a temporary car park. We park the car to the left, under the plane tree and get out to walk to the village centre. '. . .*L'anamour black and white . . .*' It's early evening and not quite dark yet. It's a great feeling. I love street parties. A bit of me which has never grown up and I hope never will, knows that this is fun. That bit takes the rest by the hand and drags it into the right mood. '. . .*Quand tu bois comme un trou . . .*'

The village square and the main street are laid out for the fun we'll be having. The restaurants along the main street are all open. The red and white check napkins look multicoloured under the festive rainbow lights. In front of us there's a small knot of people watching something intently. We join them to find out what's going on. It's a mime artist. She's pushing an enormous imaginary rock uphill. Every time she stops exhausted, for a rest and a drink, the rock rolls back down to the bottom of the hill and she has to retrieve it again. She is very good. She makes the invisible seem visible.

A tug on my sleeve means that it's time to move on. I'm dragged towards a large stage which has been erected at the far end of the square. As we move diagonally across the square we pass a young man who looks more like a tourist than a local, playing as a one man band, he's competing with the noise of a real band being blasted out by the public address system. It's an amusing sight. His actions clearly do not coincide with the sound that we are listening to. '. . . *Quand tu demandais a la ronde . . .*' I slow down as we walk past him and try to guess what tune he's playing. It's not easy. I can only make out the sound of his drum. He has symbols attached to his knees, a mouth organ, on a wire, stuck in front of his face, a guitar slung across his chest

74

a tenor saxophone hanging over his shoulder and a drum operated by his left foot by a slender piece of string which loops up over his shoulder and pulls on a hinged drumstick. What skill! Not only to have learnt how to play several different instruments but to be able to play them all simultaneously. What control! To be able to synchronise all the instruments so that they mesh in with each other. No! Wait! Hang on! It's probably *easier* to stay in synchrony on your own than when you're playing in a band with other people. Other people are usually a pain. Unless you hit it off together straight away and can read each other's minds, it takes days of practising the same song, to get in sync. '. . . *J'quitte le navire, desolee' Capitaine . . . Moi je veux revenir au port . . .*' I used to play the sax a bit myself in my late teens and early twenties. I taught myself, so I should know. I even got as far as leading a band I set up with a couple of friends and acquaintances. But you only really get into a 'groove' when you are all into the same music. It doesn't work if one of you wants to do their own thing or dominate the mood or pace of the music. '. . . *Qui m'aime, me suive . . .*' I guess that's the difference between a 'bunch of musicians' and a *real* band.

The tug this time is far more definite. It says, 'Hurry up!' We cross the square. The stage is still being set up. It looks like they have a play of some sort planned. I think to myself, 'The thing about leading a band was that you couldn't just be yourself you had to be many people at once. You had to encourage, chastise, lead, follow, even when you did not feel like it. And then there was the hassle of gaining new members or having to fill in when some one left.' '. . . *Qui et in, qui et out . . . STOP*'.

A more forceful and sustained tug and I'm dragged across the square towards the fun fair. The fun fair is made up of a merry go round, a shooting gallery, bumper cars, and a clairvoyant's tent. The shooting gallery is on the left. It's really brightly lit. I suppose they want us to be able to see what we are shooting at. Really generous! Usually they keep them dimly lit with as many shadows as is possible. I can't make out how you win but there are balloons attached to a board at the back of the stall and there are three spare rifles so I hand over my ten Francs and choose at random. I pick up the rifle on the left. It's lighter than I expected and the barrel seems to curve slightly to the right. '. . . *Elle me dishabile avec ses oeux . . .*'.

I hear some goal setting. 'Win the pink dragon.'

'Where?' I ask cautiously.

'To your left. You need three balloons.'

I fire. I aim, it doesn't help. Two shots and I still haven't hit a single balloon. Then the fluke. Three shots, three bangs in rapid succession. Three burst balloons exchanged for a pink dragon. '. . . *Joy!* . . .' A dragon which looks like it cost less than ten Francs. '. . . *Elle est faux* . . .' But so what? To one little girl, I'm a hero. '. . . *Joy!* . . .'

By now the square is filling up with dancing bodies. The melody and the chance to participate in the singing by shouting 'Joy!' at certain intervals, to coincide with the lyrics of the song, prove irresistible. In no time the restaurants are half empty and the square is half full. We are to hear that tune several more times that evening with similar results. I watch them for a while, and then a tug on my sleeve means it's time to join in and jump up and down for a while.

Now we are back at the *mas*. We are sitting at the front of the house looking over the edge at the marvellous view which now, is all lights. By comparison to the noise at the fête, this is absolute silence. It's warm and comfortable. Emily is in bed and we, the grown ups, are sitting up as if holding a wake. I am mourning my last night even though it isn't yet over. The calm I demonstrate, as I gently nurse my glass of cognac, is impressive. It is also a lie. In my heart and my mind I'm worried about tomorrow I'm worried about the challenge it will bring. Tomorrow means 'back home'. The day after tomorrow means 'no job to go back to'. Instead it promises an interview for a job. A job where I'm supposed to bring something 'new'. A job I would love to have. A job which sounds exciting, but I'm not sure what new things I can really bring to the world of Change Management. I have learnt a lot with Franck. We really *have* travelled. We have found out some of the underlying drivers for project failure but have we found them all? Have I really done what I wanted this holiday to help me to do? Am I yet in a position to *guarantee project success*?

The silence is broken by Franck's calm voice. 'I think that there is still one more to go.'

He startles me. 'What?' I ask sharply.

'One more core driver. One more underlying problem which causes projects to fail time after time after time.' Franck's voice drifts across on the evening breeze.

'How did you know that I was thinking about that?' I'm amazed. He seems to have read my mind.

'Because I was thinking about that myself,' he replies slowly, unfolding a very familiar piece of paper.

'You never stop do you?' comments Rosabeth, as she reaches over to offer us a top-up.

'No, I suppose I don't,' I reply.

'Not you. I meant Franck'. She explains and then with a wicked grin continues, 'But now I come to think of it you are as bad as each other.'

'It seems to me,' says Franck grimly, 'that we have an unhappy stakeholder.'

She can't resist the jargon. She asks, 'What's a stakeholder?'

Franck explains, And then asks, curiously. 'So why were you getting fed up with us?'

'Well, as usual, you haven't really explained to me what you were up to and why you were having your long conversations.'

In my mind I hear words from one of our earlier conversations. The one on the Island of Hyres, '*You will have problems if you tend not to manage your stakeholders.*'

'And,' she continues, 'I have no idea how far you have got or what you have achieved. Are you going to keep going all night? Have you discovered something amazing? Are you suddenly going to announce that you need to stay an extra day?'

The voice in my head shouts 'Bingo!' and almost deafens me. '*You will have unhappy stakeholders if you don't keep them up to date during the project.*' I shout excitedly. 'It works! And it seems to work for all change, change in our day-to-day lives, not just work, not just formal projects!' I explain my thoughts.

Franck's muted megaphone blares, '*You mean what we have learnt applies to managing **all** change* not just to business related projects?' And I get the feeling that he knew that all along.

Rosabeth adds in a bemused drawl. 'What's the big deal? I could have told you that if you'd asked me.'

I smile. 'I suppose you could. That's the whole problem. All the stuff we have unravelled is blindingly obvious in retrospect. It's just that it's so interwoven that we all see *part* of the picture,' I hold up the battle scarred napkin, which now looks like a Piccasso by Shakespeare, 'but not the *whole*. So we get things half right which is great. But don't forget that getting them half right also means that we get them half wrong.'

She nods. 'I see what you mean It's like having flu and taking something for the headache but not for the blocked nose. You still feel terrible.'

'And,' adds Franck, 'the pressure of your blocked nose brings the headache back after a while.'

Rosabeth's question has still not been answered so she persists, 'So how far have you got?'

I reply. I explain what we have done so far and say, 'Franck thinks that there is another core driver to all this. Don't you Franck?'

'Yes I do. Tell me, how will you feel at the end of our journey?'

I look at him not understanding why he's asked me this. I thought he knew how I felt. 'If we find all the underlying causes, I'll feel great.'

'Why?' He probes.

'Well,' I reply, 'because I'll feel that I have achieved something worthwhile.'

Franck is pointing at the bubble which says unhappy or demotivated team. 'So why do you think that we end up with an unhappy or demo-tivated team?'

Rosabeth answers before I have a chance, 'It's because, as with all you action-men, you forget to make sure that they are getting the challenges or rewards which they need or want from you. I'll bet that you even forget to talk to them during the job and occasionally say "Thanks".'

'What impact does that have?' asks Franck.

'It leaves them feeling as if they have spent all that energy and not achieved something worthwhile.' Rosabeth answers knowingly.

I protest. 'But sometimes it's not because you forget to say "Thanks". It's just that . . . Well . . . really, you can't specifically say what they have specifically contributed to the team.'

'That's really rich! You get a group of stakeholders to follow you and then you complain about what they are contributing. When you get to know as much about people as every one else, you will realise that it is very important for everyone, even the most insignificant, to have a specific role which is theirs. Even if they are required to spend most of their time mucking in. It's the only way that they can feel good about themselves and so do good work.' Rosabeth is giving me a hard time but I guess I deserve it. After all she's right.

'So,' says Franck, 'can you remember why you often don't give them a specific role?'

'Well when you start off on a project you can't really trust them to do a significant piece of work, so I guess you don't make it too clear who is responsible for what, so you can keep your hand in. But then, as the project progresses, you find that you still can't or haven't given them responsibilities . . .'

'Can't or won't?' he asks.

In my heart I know that it's more a won't than a can't, but once you've got into the habit of giving out little responsibility to team members it becomes very hard to change it. I don't feel it's really my fault so I say, 'A bit of both really.'

Franck nods. Rosabeth looks as if she doesn't really believe me. I'm starting to feel as if I am being interrogated by the thought police. In spite of the cool breeze I can feel beads of sweat forming on my fore-head. Why is it so difficult to answer such innocent looking questions? I know, if the last few conversations are anything of a guide, that at the bottom of it all we will find some cause which is down to **me**. My fault. My lack of skill. I know that already. My intuition tells me so and I don't really want to find out. But Franck has smelt blood and won't let go.

He asks, 'So your team members haven't really got a sense of what they have achieved individually because you never get round to allowing them to grow their skills and personal contributions?'

'You could say that.' I say non-committaly. He's right of course and I hate him for it. At the fête earlier in the evening, the audience had only really come alive when they were allowed to participate in the singing by shouting 'Joy!' They understood both task and role and felt great about it.

'And what do you think causes that?' he asks slowly.

I think for a while. 'Laziness?'

Franck smiles. 'I can see how that would apply in your case but I don't think it will apply to everyone.'

I'm stuck but surprisingly, for someone who has been giving me such a hard time, Rosabeth comes to my rescue. 'I've noticed,' she says thoughtfully, 'that sometimes the only way you can get people to feel responsibility is if you can either give them distinct roles or tasks.'

'What do you mean?' I ask tentatively.

'You know. It's the same whenever you have a group of people trying to achieve anything.' She's struggling to come up with an example. But she doesn't have to. I've come up with one for myself from earlier that evening. It's 'Joy!' again. It's the band.

'I see!' I exclaim. 'It's the difference between a band reading musical scores, each *on* their own (a bit like assigning tasks) and a band impro-vising. You know, one to be mellow, one to punctuate the sound (just like assigning roles.). For a *closed* project assigning ***tasks*** is probably more appropriate whilst for an *open* project **roles** are the key.'

'What's an "open" project?' asks Rosabeth.

I realise that I have slipped into jargon and explain. I end by saying. 'That means that the chunk of change needs to be described either in terms of the various jobs that obviously need to be done or by helping people to know what and when to chip in. If you have chosen inappropriate planning and co-ordination methods for the characteristics of the project you are running, the method will hide the fact that you have failed to pass bits to the team and you will continue through the project in blissful ignorance.'

Franck has been silent throughout my monologue. He looks at me and asks silently. 'What are the implications of what you have just said?'

'Well,' I say. I'm starting to really cook now. 'Well, it helps explain why, as the project proceeds it can be so difficult to use the team fully or allow them to grow their skills.'

'Anything else?'

'Yes. It means that other team members have little sense of what their colleagues are contributing. This makes it hard for them to appreciate each other's contributions or reward each other.'

'There is another one,' he says quietly, 'quite devastating.'

'What?' I demand. As usual my brain has gone on vacation.

'Oh yes, I see it,' says Rosabeth, 'If you don't work out the tasks or roles you require and assign them, it gets very difficult to establish if people have the skills needed. This means that you cannot justify training them and you will end up with an untrained team who do not have the skills or expertise for the change you are asking them to implement.'

I latch on and add, 'And they will makes errors or do things which they shouldn't be doing. Having a whole person who spends half their time on things irrelevant to project progress is like having half a person who spends all their time on things relevant to project progress. The overall effect is that you will be under-resourced. And we know what simultaneously being under-resourced and making errors means.' I pause for effect. 'It means a failure to meet the hard objectives of the project and it means unhappy and demotivated stakeholders.'

Franck is leaning towards me listening intently. 'Keep digging,' he encourages.

'You mean why do I not assign roles and tasks and grow my team?'

Franck nods.

I know the answer but I don't really want to say it. I hate delegating. I'm usually worried that I will lose control and well, you know the feeling. While I'm dithering Franck reads my mind and answers for me.

'You hate delegating don't you?'

'Well you've never been there. In the real world the project leader carries all the responsibility. You just can't trust it to anybody.'

'Especially if you don't know how to manage a team.'

'Er, yes.'

Then the muted megaphone. *'Anyone who doesn't understand how a team forms; how it functions; how it moves from being a group of people with differing objectives to being a team; how you get them to follow your lead, so that things get done even when no instructions are issued, is going to find it pretty difficult to delegate.* Tell me what are the other implications of not knowing how to lead a team?'

I reply speaking slowly, as if each word is a delicious morsel which I wish to savour. 'If you don't understand how to lead a team, if you have never seen a team really functioning then I agree that it would be very foolish to delegate. If you don't understand how to lead a team, and if you delegate then things would certainly not go as you wished. It would happen like this: first, what would happen would be that you would lose control. *People create change* but not the change required. They will also *constrain change*, and knowing Murphy's Law it is bound to be precisely the change which is actually required.'

Rosabeth is watching me intently. I think she is trying to make up her mind whether I'm guessing or actually thinking it through.

I hate having someone hanging so closely onto my words. It makes me nervous and even more hesitant, but I ignore her and continue. 'If you didn't know how to lead a team then when, quite naturally, the project starts to go astray you will not have understood the feelings of the team and you will not have distinguished their behaviours and you will not be able to stop behaviour which did not lead towards project success. So things would certainly not go as you wished.'

I pause. The night air is still. Below us the scattered lights shine deeply against the dark background of the earth. Just below and just above the horizon it is much brighter. Two moons, one round, one in shimmering slices, shine boldly at us, as if daring me to have the courage to go to the end of my thoughts. It's delicious. I can almost feel that job falling into my lap. Maybe I do have something to contribute. To my knowledge, this is the first time that all the spaghetti, confusing the change process and how projects work, has ever been unravelled. Maybe I can change project management from a black art of luck and happenstance into a science. The science of *managing **all change***. *Managing all change in chunks, project by project.* I take my time and then I say the word myself, to myself, softly.

'Why?'

And I answer myself '***Because I have never really understood the skills and personal qualities required for leading people***. A person who leads others to change, acts as a guide and a builder. Acts to make things, which have not yet happened, seem possible. Acts to make the invisible seem visible. Acts as though they understand the innermost needs of all the individuals they lead. Acts realising that the thoughts and feelings of individuals are not the thoughts and feelings of a team. Acts with sincerity and trustworthiness. If you lack sincerity and trustworthiness in what you say and what you do and rely on authority and power alone, who in the world can or will follow you? After all, with change which is sequential, change which alters with time, you will never have power and authority over all your stakeholders. Such a person builds groups of followers into teams which act as a single body. Builds stakeholders into advocates and supporters.'

I pause but my audience is silent. So I carry on, 'If you don't understand the skill and art of working with and leading people and ignore stakeholder balancing you will find it almost impossible to get the commitment you need from specialists or senior management with all the knock-on problems that that causes.'

Franck raises his hand triumphantly in a half salute and says, 'Number four!'

'Is that it?' I ask relieved and elated.

'I think so,' he replies.

'So do I.' Rosabeth passes me the cognac. I top up our glasses. It's magical. I think I've done it. I mean we've done it. I mean Franck has guided me there. *To succeed in all change you manage it in chunks, a project at a time. You don't have to spend twenty years learning snippets which confuse rather than enlighten. There are **only four core skills** which you need to have in order to significantly increase your chances of success in managing change in chunks.*

I raise my glass 'To tomorrow.'

'To projects and chunks.'

'To all change.'

Chapter 10

DOWN THE CREEK
WITHOUT A PADDLE

'Congratulations!'
I'm feeling rather pleased with myself.
'To win such a large contract, and to win over two global consultancies and one International Business School! How did you do it?'

'I just talked about change. I talked about it in a realistic common-sense way. I explained the first four laws of change and explained how we applied them to all change and then I talked about the skills groupings for their *project leaders*. Oops! I mean *change agents*. That's what they insist on calling them.'

I'm sitting in my new office talking to Cathy. The two months since I joined her organisation have simply flown by. I say in a worried voice. 'Our real problem is the number of people they want us to work with.'

Cathy appears not to have understood the tone of my voice. She seems to think that I am less than keen but interprets this as normal business apprehension. She insists. 'It's good business though isn't it?'

'Yes. I agree.' I try to explain my reservations more clearly. I'm worried that there is too big a gap between my/our knowledge of change management and theirs. I'm worried that they will hear what we say, but not understand it. I'm worried that we will take the few who work closely with us along at a rate too fast for the others to keep up and leave them more confused and divided than they are now. I know that unless we can provide a method for **all** of them to learn at the same rate, unless we can provide a rate faster than our direct involvement alone allows I am not sure that they will turn around fast enough. The thoughts are rushing into my brain. I am not sure if they will turn around at all. They will simply start changes in the organisation. **Changes** which are **not improvements**. And I know that since *one change leads to another*, the changes have a chance of snowballing. And since the changes they start with will not improve anything, they will add more changes. And since *adding change to change creates chaos*, their organisation will get increasingly chaotic. Less and less able to cope with the pressures it's facing. Indeed instead of helping them succeed, we will be helping them commit corporate suicide.

I know all this and yet as usual my brain deserts me. Instead of explaining all this; instead of helping Cathy to understand what I understand; instead of articulating my thoughts; my statement, 'Yes. I agree,' is followed by a pause, a long, 'er'. And then I say, 'It's a big job. I think I need more resources.'

'I see what you mean,' she says. 'I shall think about it. Why don't you raise it at the partners' meeting tomorrow?'

I nod in agreement. It's a lie. I know in my heart and mind that the partners' meeting will not solve anything. I try to smile confidently. I want her to think that I know what I'm up to. She smiles back. A warm friendly smile. Just like her voice. A smile you just can't help liking. I grin. She gets up and walks to the door. As she turns the handle a leather clad courier practically falls into the room carrying a brown parcel. 'Sorry,' he mumbles in apology to Cathy but he is too late. She is already gone. He looks directly at me and says, 'They said downstairs that I would find you here. Please sign.' First he hands me a form to sign and then passes me the parcel.

As I take the parcel the 'phone starts to ring. I walk back behind my desk throwing a farewell over my shoulder. 'Bye.'

Now it's early evening. It's quiet. I think most people have left. The afternoon has been pretty hectic but not fruitful. It looks as if my ability to sell has just about dropped me in it. It's one thing to outsell your competitors by talking to them about your latest ideas but it's another thing altogether to find enough of the right resource to help you deliver your promises. I have raised the stakeholders' expectations but can not get anyone who will or can follow my lead, so that we can deliver what has been promised. I have spent the afternoon trying to convince colleagues and contacts. Their reactions are similar if not the same. 'I'd love to help, it sounds really interesting' and 'it looks as if you have found out something I had not understood and would love to learn but I can't see how you can train me up to get me up to speed in time for me to do a competent job. Sorry. I can't help.' What a frustrating afternoon.

I'm packing up to go home when I notice the package still unopened on my desk. I've never been able to resist opening packages. The kid in me I guess. I find opening parcels reminds me of the warm and fulfilled feelings of early Christmases, when I still believed there was a Santa. It pulls me back to the times before now. The times when you couldn't just go out and buy what you wanted when you wanted. Instead you had to wait for an annual event, a birthday, to receive the objects of your desire, gift wrapped. I reach over and peel off the adhesive tape and

Woodforde,
26 Konnoongana St. Brisbane.
23 October

Hello Mate!

Got Your letter telling me your good news, good to see that you can still con your way into anything. You should be ashamed of yourself. My guess is that by now you are at the stage where you have told everyone about your discoveries and they are getting very interested but your audience is bigger than you can handle. Am I right? Call me an angel sent to deliver you. I have attached a copy of the manuscript for my next book. It's a sort of handbook for people who want to manage projects or chunks of change. Use it yourself and pass it on if you must but tell whoever you give it to, to be discreet about having it. If my publisher finds out that I have given away a copy of the manuscript he will kill me. This is our secret.

Good luck!   Franck

unwrap it. It is a two inch high stack of paper. There is a hand-written letter on the top.

That's just typical of Franck. Out-thinking me and being just one step ahead. Nice thought but as usual he is ahead of me. I start off miffed and then the realisation dawns. 'What is my biggest problem? It's spreading the ideas we developed in France widely and quickly.' I get this warm feeling. 'If it's any good I should be able to overcome my difficulty in spreading our ideas and thoughts on **managing all change by parcelling it up into projects or chunks**. This manuscript may be what I need to fulfill the volume of work I have just sold.' I lift the two inch pile of paper and place it squarely in front of me. I twist the desk lamp round to shine directly onto it, turn the first page and start to read.

THE
PROJECT
LEADER'S
SECRET
HANDBOOK

How to use this handbook

This handbook is in three parts; called **Diagnosing your own project, Try these** and **All those new words**. The first part diagnoses your project and identifies the types of issues you are facing and what skills and behaviours you need to learn most urgently. The second part is split up under four headings. The four headings are the four groups of skills, knowledge and behaviours that you will need to have to stand the best chance of success. A number of methods, tools and frameworks are described in each part. The third part called, 'All those new words' is a glossary of all the unfamiliar words used in the story and the handbook. You should refer to this part if the jargon starts to baffle you.

Once you have completed your diagnosis you will be directed to the most appropriate parts in the second part in sequence.

If you do not have a project to diagnose then simply read through the second part in sequence.

Contents

Part 1

DIAGNOSING YOUR OWN PROJECT OR CHUNK OF CHANGE

This part helps you determine the issues you face with your particular project or chunk of change (as I call it) and helps to customise the use of the other two parts of the handbook section specifically to meet your individual needs.

Section 1.1
IS IT WORTH DOING?

Have you ever thought to yourself during or at the end of a project you have done or that someone else has done, 'What a waste of time'? My bet is that you have. Why does this happen over and over again? My guess is that it happens as a result of three common causes. Sometimes you are fire fighting and the project is not thought through properly. After all who has time to think when there is a fire raging? So despite your tremendous effort, no sooner have you damped down the flames at the top of the inferno than they are re-lit by the hot ashes underneath. Sometimes you actually succeed with the change you were planning but unfortunately the outcome is not exactly what you wanted. The result does little to help you towards your original goals. It may instead, move you away from them. It may not be adopted by the people who are supposed to live with it. Sometimes you actually get it right. You should be delighted, only someone has moved the goal posts. The world has changed.

Tell me about the project you are thinking about as you read this book. *Why* is it being done?

The First Law of Change says *one change leads to another*. If that's true, then any change is only to be undertaken under **extreme** need. After all, doing projects for the 'heck of it' is bound to lead to a further need for a response of some sort. And I am sure that you don't want to end up with the chaos suggested by the second law. A project **must only be undertaken to solve a problem**. I see you nod. I agree too. But what is a problem? Is a problem simply something that you don't like? I've said it. You've said it, 'I've got a really big problem.'

A QUICK QUIZ

Which of these is a problem?
1. I'm out of a job again.
2. I'm stuck behind a lorry which is crawling up a steep hill.
3. I've just spent 250 Francs on a phone call.
4. I'm sipping a cocktail called Blue Lagoon.

Answer:

All or none or any.

A problem is something which gets in the way of achieving your goals. Since the goals are not specified you can't say which is a problem. This is not a silly semantic argument though. If problems are things that get in the way of achieving your goals, then unless you have goals, you do not have any problems! (And if you don't know what your goals are, then you do not realise all the problems you actually have!)

It is important to define the overall goals. It is from them that you know what problems you actually have. And it's the problems which give rise to the need to manage changes to put them right. (Some people who are more optimistic than I am, prefer the use of the word '*opportunity*' rather than the word '*problem*'. If you are an optimist, read the sentence above as: **An opportunity is a route to achieving your goals**.

ANOTHER QUICK QUIZ

See if you can fill this in over the next three minutes.

a. The goal of my organisation is:

....

b. A barrier to reaching the goal (or for you optimists; a route to reach the goal) is:

....

....

....

....

....

....

c. The chunk of change required to overcome this barrier (provide this route) is:

....

....

....

....

....

....

....

....

d. I am certain that this is the **correct** and **minimum** amount of change I need to carry out because . . .

....

....

....

....

....

Scoring

Per answer
a. 10 points b. 10 points. c. 10 points d. 10 points

Subtract ten points for every ten seconds by which you overran the three minutes you had to answer the questions.

Total = ...

If you scored less than 10 points you may wish to consider putting your project on hold until you are sure that it is worth doing.

Section 1.2
WHAT TYPE OF CHANGE IS IT?

SYMPTOM CHECK 1

Please tick *at least one* statement in each row. If two statements are the same tick both.

Our organisation has *little* experience of this type of change.	Our organisation has *some* experience of this type of change.	Our organisation has *some* experience of this type of change.	Our organisation has *lots* of experience of this type of change.
Our organisation is *not able to change* as fast as the external world (competitors, customer needs, Governmental and legislative requirements, etc.)	Our organisation is *barely able to change* as fast as the external world (competitors, customer needs, Governmental and legislative requirements, etc.)	Our organisation is *just able to change* as fast as the external world (competitors, customer needs, Governmental or legislative requirements, etc.)	Our organisation is *well able to change* faster than the external world (competitors, customers needs, Governmental or legislative requirements, etc.)
Our organisation has been caught off guard and has been surprised by *many* of the changes it has had to face recently.	Our organisation has been caught off guard and has been surprised by *some* of the changes it has had to face recently.	Our organisation has been caught off guard and has been surprised by *some* of the changes it has had to face recently.	Our organisation has been caught off guard or has been surprised by *few* of the changes it has had to face recently.
Our organisation is trying to implement a new strategy.	Our organisation is trying to continue a new strategy.	Our organisation is trying to continue an existing strategy.	Our organisation is implementing a long established strategy.
We *don't know* where to go *but can't stay here*.	We *know* where to go *but getting there looks demanding*.	We *know* where to go *but don't know how*.	We *need to do more of the same in slightly different conditions*.
I can list *almost none* of the tasks I need to carry out.	I can list *a few* of the tasks I need to carry out.	I can list *some* of the tasks I need to carry out.	I can list *almost all* of the tasks I need to carry out.
I *do not really* understand the methods and processes which I will be using during the project.	I *fully* understand the methods and processes which I will be using during the project.	I *have some idea* of the methods and processes which I will be using during the project.	I *fully* understand the methods and processes which I will be using during the project.

Column totals

97

Please tick *at least one word in each row* which describes best how you feel about your project.

confused	purposeful	challenged	confident
lost	open	convinced	small
frightened	spoilt for choice	excited	organised
groping	choosy	purposeful	challenged
thrown	capable	questing	competent
bewildered	competent	searching	stretched
confounded	adept	casting about	clear
fuddled	proficient	single minded	complex

Column totals

Solution

1. For *both* tables of the symptom check, please add up the number of ticks in each *vertical* column.

2. Add the totals for both tables together and record them below.

Totals

       F_____   **M**_____   **Q**_____   **P**_____

3. Please select the letter/code which has the highest score and circle it.

What does this mean?

As we saw in Chapter Seven, projects come in four types. The quiz above helps identify the type of concept behind your project.

F – the Walking or Lost in the **Fog** type of project is formally known as an *open project*. If you are running one you really feel as if you are caught in the fog. You can't stay where you are, so you've got to move. You are walking in a thick, but uneven fog. In *open* projects you, and most of your stakeholders, are *unsure of what* is to be done and *unsure of how* it is to be carried out. Typically the organisation is attempting to do something that it has never attempted before. This is usually because the external business, political, legislative or sociological environment has changed or because the organisation is implementing a new part of its strategy.

An example would be running a Quality Improvement programme for the first time or developing a brand new product for a market or segment which you have not sold to in the past.

The secret of success in this type of project is to proceed very carefully, to proceed one step at a time.

M – the Making a **Movie** type of project is formally known as a *semi-open project*. In *semi-open* projects you and most of your stakeholders are *very sure of how* the project should be conducted but *not of what* is to be done. Typically the organisation has built up significant expertise and investment in the methods it intends to apply and has several people very committed to the method. The 'There must be something we can do with our spare factory capacity,' type of problem.

An example of this is a project to develop new products or market uses for a new invention or technology. It's the typical experience an inventor goes through looking for applications for a new technology.

Because you know how the project is to be run, it is tempting to spend your time on the defining and planning – the how part of the project. (We saw in Chapter One that the professor was more interested in making use of his equipment than in what the project was to achieve.) You must instead put tremendous effort into finding yourself a good script and the movie will write itself.

Q – the Going on a **Quest** type of project is formally known as a *semi-closed* project. In *semi-closed* projects you and most of your stakeholders are *very sure of what* should be done. It is usually a very seductive idea. 'Wouldn't it be great if we could have a paperless office?' or 'If only we could have a paperless office . . . it would solve all our problems.' However, you are *unsure of how* to achieve this.

An example of this is a computerised management information system designed to present all required management information at the touch of a button.

The secret of a successful quest is to get your knights fired up and then send them off to 'seek' in parallel, different places at the same time, returning on a fixed date to report progress and share it with others.

P – The **Painting-by-numbers** type of project is formally known as a *closed* project. In closed projects you and most of your stakeholders are *sure of both what to do and how* it is to be done. These projects arise when the organisation is repeating a change of which it has significant experience. Usually each person has specific skills and you know at the outset exactly which skills are going to be required. The organisation will usually have written methods, procedures and systems describing what and how things were done in the past.

Examples of this are; a pharmaceutical company carrying out drug trials on another new substance, or an established construction company putting up yet another building.

Closed projects are difficult because since the organisation knows both what and how the project is to be carried out, the projects tend to be large, involved and very complex. The challenge is to do it better, faster, bigger or with less resources than last time.

The secret with these types of projects is to spend care and effort in drawing out the outline and numbering each shape and then painting in the right order, light colours first, and checking that everyone paints right up to the line perfectly.

Has the symptom check worked? Has it established the type of project which you're attempting to manage? Which type is it?

INDIVIDUAL TAILORING

If your project is so large that if it fails the whole organisation fails, or if falls directly out of a strategy that your organisation is following, it is known as a Strategic Project. Strategic projects have some very different additional characteristics. If you wish to read more about them have a look at the list of books in the reference section.

SYMPTOM CHECK 2

Please tick the statement in each row which best describes your project. You must tick at least one.

Progress in *almost all* aspects of the project is obvious to me.	Progress in *many* aspects of the project is *not* obvious to me.
Progress in *almost all* aspects of the project is obvious to the core team.	Progress in *many* aspects of the project is *not* obvious to the core team.
Progress in *almost all* aspects of the project is obvious to most stakeholders.	Progress in *many* aspects of the project is *not* obvious to most stakeholders.
Progress in *almost all* aspects of the project is easily measurable.	Progress in *many* aspects of the project is *not* easily measurable.
Progress in *almost all* aspects of the project is easy to report on.	Progress in *many* aspects of the project is *not* easy to report on.

Solution

1. Please add up the number of ticks in each vertical column.

Totals

V_____   **I**_____

2. Please select the letter/code which has the highest score and circle it.

What does this mean?

Chapter Six began to explain how some projects are easier to follow than others. Some have very concrete outcomes to the activities whilst others have very abstract outcomes. The quiz above helps to distinguish the two types.

V – Visible projects have very *concrete* activities and outcomes to each step as it progresses. Usually the change affects *materials*. It is very obvious to everyone – all the stakeholders – that progress is being made and it is easy to track progress to schedule.

Examples of this would be a road building project, an office relocation, or a computer network installation. There is only one time when you wish that the visible progress of your project was in fact invisible. Can you guess when? It's when something goes wrong. People running visible projects often hide spare resources, say in a different budget, or create spare time or cost by inflating estimates. This practice is a major barrier to learning how to run the next project better or to obtaining actual costs and time scales so that you can work out whether the project was really worthwhile. It is much less detrimental to stage manage what stakeholders see (like

101

organising site visits at certain times and banning stakeholders from the site at all other times).

I – Invisible projects tend to have activities and outcomes which are *abstract*. Usually the change affects *people or information* flows. The project results in changes such as changes in behaviour or attitude, or which are information based. The changes are not obvious to everyone and are often not even obvious to the people who are carrying them out. (See Chapter One on the *Locos*).

Examples would be a culture change project, a design feasibility study, a software development programme. Invisible projects are great for giving stakeholders surprises. Because they can not see the change coming it tends to come as a shock when it arrives, and they say things like, 'I didn't know that was going on or I would have told you what I wanted.' It may also become difficult to get people to appreciate all the effort you and the project team have been putting in. Instead of saying, 'Well done!', they say things like 'What happened to that thing we were doing on European sales opportunities? I'm sure *someone* was looking at that.' Or worse, it becomes near impossible to keep your current resources or get more if they are needed, because after all, 'You've been working on it for some time and we haven't seen much progress.'

SYMPTOM CHECK 3

Please tick the statement(s) in each row which best describes your project. If a statement is repeated please tick it twice.

Most of the money spent is internally transferred 'funny money'.	Most of the money spent has been provided by our organisation and one or several others.	Most of the money spent is 'real' money we have passed on to another organisation.	Our organisation is being paid 'real' money for the work being done on the project.
Most of the resources used in the project are provided by our organisation.	Most of the resources used in the project are provided by our organisation and one or several others.	Most of the resources used in the project are provided by another organisation.	Most of the resources used in the project are provided by our organisation but charged out.
The organisation which will live with the outcome of the change *is the same* as the organisation carrying out the change (might be a different department or division but same financial entity). It is *my* organisation.	The organisation which will live with the outcome of the change *is one or several* of the organisations responsible for carrying out the change.	The organisation which will live with the outcome of the change *is my* organisation. It *is not* the organisation responsible for carrying out most of the change.	The organisation which will live with the outcome is *not my* organisation. My organisation is responsible for carrying out most of the change.
Many of the most influential stakeholders are in the same organisation as I am.	Many of the most influential stakeholders are in the same organisation as I am.	Many of the most influential stakeholders are *not* in the same organisation as I am.	Many of the most influential stakeholders are *not* in the same organisation as I am.
I am very concerned about internal politics and how it affects the way I lead the project.	I am very concerned about internal politics and how it affects the way I lead the project.	I am *not* very concerned about internal politics and how it affects the way I lead the project.	I am *not* very concerned about internal politics and how it affects the way I lead the project.
For most of the project activities there are *no* legal contractual agreements.	For most of the project activities there are *no* legal contractual agreements.	For most of the project activities there are legal contractual agreements.	For most of the project activities there are legal contractual agreements.
Totals			
C_____	J_____	T_____	E_____

Solution

1. Please add up the number of ticks in each vertical column.

2. Please select the letter/code which has the highest score and circle it.

What does this mean?

As we saw in Chapter Seven: So similar . . . Yet so different, human beings respond to change in different ways depending on whether they are doing it to themselves or whether it is being done to them. As a result, the position, accessibility and power of the outcome stakeholders with respect to the project leader and the core team has a significant effect on the ease or difficulty of stakeholder balancing and the relative measures of project success. It determines the way in which the outcome stakeholders drive the project and also the level of ownership and responsibility felt for the project, not only by the outcome stakeholders, but also by the core team responsible for delivery.

C – Change projects are *internal* projects. The main outcome stakeholders are in the same organisation as the project leader. They are The Client of the project, who has to live with the outcome of the project, is the project leader's own organisation. This makes the project *internally driven*. The organisation responsible for the delivery of the project is the project leader's organisation. The stakeholders responsible for delivery, the core team, and the invisible team are also in the same organisation, so they are also *internally delivered*. Change projects are projects run by the organisation, for itself.

Examples are cost cutting initiatives, office moves, new product or service developments. Internal projects are usually severely influenced by the internal politics of the various functions or department which have a stakeholding in the project. The project leader's ability to influence is dependent on whether s/he or the sponsor belong(ed) to a department function or division which is powerful in the organisation.

J – Collaborative projects or Joint Ventures are a *hybrid* type of project. The project is *internally driven* but the project leader's organisation is only one of the organisations with important outcome stakeholders. This makes it *externally driven* as well. Often the project leader does not even belong to any of the organisations which have the major outcome stakeholders. The project is also often *internally and externally delivered*. Both the project leader's organisation and other organisations are responsible for the delivery of the project. Such projects are notoriously difficult to manage because they demonstrate all the worst characteristics of all the other three types. Each joint venture partner brings with them all the elements of an internal project. In addition there are all the financial and contractual issues relating to commercial projects.

T – Turnkey or ContracT projects occur when the project is *internally driven* and *externally delivered*. The project leader belongs to the organisation which is responsible for defining and driving the project but not for its delivery.

Examples of this type of project are office refurbishment, market research projects, external training courses, consultancy assignments. As project leader you may find yourself placed in a position of policeman: a position which you must not accept. Accepting the role of policeman usually leads to a low-trust relationship being established. The low-trust relationship has its own dynamic which tends to work to the detriment of the completion of the project. Project leader: 'I don't trust them so I shall keep an eye on them and check on them regularly.' Contractor: 'The project leader has been sniffing around again. S/he is obviously looking for something to "beat us up" with. Whatever we do we must keep everything as secret and close to our chests as possible.' Project leader: 'This contractor is not very open. They must have something to hide. I shall need to check on them even more closely.' And so on.

E – CommErcial projects are projects run to *make money* **directly** from the project itself. These projects are *externally driven* by the client organisation (the organisation which will be parting with the money). Since the organisation which has to live with the change is also the organisation parting with the money this gives them a complete right to drive the project. *Delivery is internal*. The project leader's own organisation is responsible for the delivery of the project. Because of the financial agreements involved it is common to have legally binding contractual agreements.

Examples of commercial projects generally relate to organisations who sell complex or bespoke products or services. Consultancy projects and construction or development projects, specialist engineering products fall into this category. This type of project has several natural tensions built into it. The project leader's organisation is attempting to complete the project without itself having spent all the money it receives on the delivery of the project. The client organisation is keen for the project to succeed but not necessarily at any cost. To add to this, **all** the stakeholders in the client organisation, no matter how remote, feel that they have a right to influence the project because, 'We are paying for it.' As project leader, this may not match with your ranking of stakeholder importance and you may find balancing their expectations difficult.

Section 1.3
WHAT SORT OF PROBLEMS SHOULD YOU EXPECT?

I'd love to know what sort of project yours has turned out to be. You may wish to record what you have discovered below.

Are you?	Are your activities?	Are you driving/delivering a:
Painting-by-numbers ____	**V**isible _____	**C**hange Project _____
Making a **M**ovie _____	**I**nvisible _____	**J**oint Venture _____
Going on a **Q**uest _____		**T**urnkey Project _____
Walking in the **F**og _____		Comm**E**rcial Project _____

CRYSTAL BALL GAZING

There is an exercise that I often get my course delegates to carry out which I call 'crystal ball gazing'. It is my attempt to help them get a sense of perspective and to get them into the habits of an 'ideal' person, a person who 'thinks of trouble and prevents it'. I try to get them to realise that once *you understand project types* and can *predict the problems* then you **do *not* have to live through the problems**.

I put them in pairs and then I ask them to work out the type characteristics of their own projects. They then write this down on a piece of paper and swap it with their partner. **Without knowing any of the details or content** of the project the partner then has to guess:

- The issues and problems that they have had with the project so far and what was easy to do.
- The problems and issues that they currently have and what is going well.
- The issues and problems that they are likely to have in the future.

These are to be answered with regard to the stakeholders (sponsor, client, core team, invisible team, other stakeholders) and the hard criteria (financial cost or returns, timeliness, competitive advantage, specifications or quality).

I'll give you a chance to try crystal ball gazing. Here goes. I have a project which is a closed, painting-by-numbers project which is largely invisible and is being driven by my commercial needs. The code for this would be **P – I – E**.

106

YET ANOTHER QUICK QUIZ

In each pair choose the statement which best describes what I am experiencing **now**.

a. The sponsor doesn't understand what the project is all about.
b. The sponsor keeps suggesting things I should be doing.

a. I am completely sure of where we are up to and so is my sponsor.
b. I am worried that I can't really keep tabs on progress in some parts of the project and my sponsor thinks that I might be losing control.

a. The client is well aware of what is going on without me having to spend much time updating them.
b. The client keeps asking for meetings. At the meetings most time is spent trying to establish what we have done.

a. The client is working closely with us on a day-to-day basis.
b. The client has an audit group who checks our work.

a. The roles of the core team have been developing through the project. Even now they are still evolving.
b. The core team have a good understanding of what is required of them.

a. I have had to work hard to agree a reimbursable contract.
b. The core team are fed up with me harping on about budgets

a. People seem happy to do favours for me with no payback to them.
b. People are unwilling to do favours for me.

a. Some department heads are trying to get back the people and resources I have gathered for the project.
b. People seem not to realise how much business I am responsible for.

a. The end users know what they are going to get and seem happy about it.
b. The end users are complaining that they had comments to make about the design and hadn't realised how far we had got.

a. I am keeping a very close eye on the hourly cost figures for the project.
b. I am keeping a very close eye on both the actual work which has been done, the hourly cost figures and the total related spend.

a. I am trying to complete early.
b. I am struggling to complete to schedule.

a. I am totally fed up with all the changes to specification. They keep inventing new factors.
b. There aren't too many specification changes, and anyway we make money on the contract with each spec. change. It's the negotiations which take up

my time. That and trying to discover if one of my team hasn't taken it on themselves to satisfy the client without telling me.

Scoring

Score a. No points for each answer a.   b. One point for each answer b.

a. _____   b. _____

What does this mean?

If you scored more than eight have a go at crystal ball gazing yourself. Work on a change activity which is important to you. I have put three pages at the end of this section for you to work on.

If you scored less than eight, I suggest that you re-read the section.

GAZING INTO THE *PAST*

The Stakeholders

sponsor _____

client _____

core team _____

invisible team _____

end users _____

other stakeholders _____

Hard criteria

financial cost or returns _____

timeliness _____

competitive advantage
specifications or quality _____

GAZING INTO THE *PRESENT*

The Stakeholders

sponsor _____

client _____

core team _____

invisible team _____

end users _____

other stakeholders _____

Hard criteria

financial cost or returns _____

timeliness _____

competitive advantage
specifications or quality _____

GAZING INTO THE *FUTURE*

The Stakeholders

sponsor _____

client _____

core team _____

invisible team _____

end users _____

other stakeholders _____

Hard criteria

financial cost or returns _____

timeliness _____

competitive advantage
specifications or quality _____

Section 1.4
WHICH BUBBLES (SKILLS/TOOLS) SHOULD YOU FOCUS ON?

If you have succeeded in correctly diagnosing your chunk of change, you may wish to go through Part Two in an order which gives you answers to your problems in the most relevant way to your immediate needs. The table below tells you in which order to go through Part Two.

Type of Chunk	Walking in the Fog	Making a Movie	Going on a Quest	Painting-by-Numbers
Section Learning to Learn (Section 2.1)	First	Second	Fourth	Fourth
Managing Stakeholders (Section 2.2)	Third	First	Third	First
Planning and Co-ordination (Section 2.3)	Fourth	Fourth	Second	Second
Working with and Leading People (Section 2.4)	Second	Third	First	Third

Part 2
TRY THESE

By and large it is our failures which civilise us.
Our successes merely confirm our bad habits.
Clive James

This section introduces some of the main thinking, skills and behaviour frameworks which you can use to help you in developing your successful career managing change in chunks. They relate to the core problems that we discovered. ***I've used them myself, so I know that they work***. I must however warn you that becoming competent at using these tools is very dangerous. When you can clearly see what needs to be done you may become impatient to see its outcome. This is where your problem starts. Others around you, your key stakeholders, may not have such clarity. Usually they will not understand what you are suggesting and may even go so far as to suggest that you are wrong! You have Mother Nature to blame, don't forget that learning and understanding are biological processes. To truly change the way another person thinks takes reinforcement over several months. After which they may approach you and repeat what you suggested, often in your own words, and insist that it's their latest idea.

I recommend Patience and Humility, two qualities which I have never possessed but have sometimes been able to fake.

Section 2.1
LEARNING TO LEARN

What is the real Goal? . . . To teach the world to learn.
Eliyahu M. Goldratt

A QUICK TEST

Below are nine sets of four words. Rank the words which best characterise the way in which you try to make sense of what is going on in the world around you. Use a scale of 1, 2, 3 and 4. For each row, score as **4** the word which **best** characterises your style and as **1** the one which **least** characterises your style.

You may find it hard to choose between words. There are no right or wrong answers so just choose the one that feels right.

1. discriminating_____ tentative_____ involved_____ practical_____

2. receptive_____ relevant_____ analytical_____ impartial_____

3. feeling_____ watching_____ thinking_____ doing_____

4. accepting_____ risk taker_____ evaluative_____ aware_____

5. intuitive_____ productive_____ logical_____ questioning_____

6. abstract_____ observing_____ concrete_____ active_____

7. present oriented_____ reflecting_____ future oriented_____ pragmatic_____

8. experience_____ observation__ conceptualization_ experimentation_

9. intense_____ reserved_____ rational_____ responsible_____

(See References Learning Styles Questionnaire, Kolb)

In recent years it has become increasingly trendy to talk about learning. There are published articles and even books on what is called 'organisational learning'. But what is meant by learning? I think that learning is a series of steps which we go through in order to make better sense of the world around us and to better prepare us for problems which may arise in the future. I believe that once we have learnt something, for a while it takes conscious effort to remember it and apply what we have learnt. However, after we have repeated the thoughts and actions several times, carrying out what we have learnt, it becomes increasingly difficult to notice what we are doing or even to think our way through in the same painstaking step-by-step fashion which we used at first. The thing that we have learnt slowly moves into our subconscious and becomes a habit – something that we do or think automatically.

I learnt how to fly a glider long after I learnt how to drive a car. I understood a lot about the learning process by the act of trying to get a driving licence. I understood even more about it from trying to learn to fly.

Do you remember your first driving lesson? Most people don't. They just remember vaguely what it felt like. I would like to take you through the whole experience in slow motion, step-by-step. It will help illustrate what I mean by the learning process.

Imagine yourself climbing into the driver's seat for the first time. It feels strange for a start, you have to ease yourself behind the steering wheel. Knobs and dials which you previously only recognised from an oblique angle now stare you fully in the face. You square up to them as your instructor tells you to 'Adjust it so that it feels comfortable.' But what is 'Comfortable?' You've never done this before, you don't know what to look for, so you ask 'How far back should it go?' And the answer comes back. 'So that you can push the pedals all the way down' This sounds like good advice but doesn't really help. After all do you push the pedals with your legs straight or bent?

The main controls are then pointed out to you and explained. This of course, is a complete waste of your time, since at that point, you have no idea how they actually interact with you once you start driving. Eventually, you are allowed to turn the key in the ignition. The engine roars to life. The noise you hear is certainly louder than you have ever heard it before. Your immediate reaction is 'What the !!!!!' but you remember the discussion about 'pushing the pedals all the way down' and realise that your foot is hard down on the pedal on the right (what experienced drivers call the accelerator). Your guess is that this is the cause of the noise. So you experiment, you lift your foot up all the way and the noise of the over-revving engine dies down. Some readers may not have had a chance to go through this process themselves. Their instructor may have promptly but firmly instructed them to, 'Get your *@!*$ foot off the !!*&%$! accelerator.' Either way, once the sound has died away to a dull rumble there is a real temptation to push one's foot down slightly, 'Just to see if it gets noisy again.' You need to do this to complete the cycle because if it does, then you can firmly establish in your mind the link between the position of your foot and the previously revving engine. Figure 2.1 illustrates this process.

115

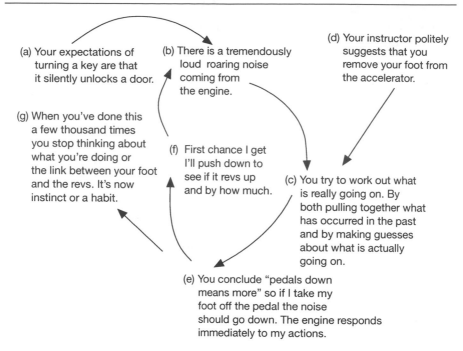

(a) Your expectations of turning a key are that it silently unlocks a door.

(b) There is a tremendously loud roaring noise coming from the engine.

(d) Your instructor politely suggests that you remove your foot from the accelerator.

(g) When you've done this a few thousand times you stop thinking about what you're doing or the link between your foot and the revs. It's now instinct or a habit.

(f) First chance I get I'll push down to see if it revs up and by how much.

(c) You try to work out what is really going on. By both pulling together what has occurred in the past and by making guesses about what is actually going on.

(e) You conclude "pedals down means more" so if I take my foot off the pedal the noise should go down. The engine responds immediately to my actions.

Fig. 2.1 The Learning Cycle, Part 1 – The Practice

The four steps in the middle (b, c, e and f) are known as the *first hand* learning cycle. First hand because the opportunity arises from things you experience yourself, that is, first hand. I have added the bits on the outside (a, d and g) to complete the picture. You see, to learn from any experience that you experience first hand, you need to be capable of going through all four steps. You can also learn second hand. (Look at the top right hand ring.) The suggestion, made by your instructor, is an opportunity to use something which someone else has learnt to solve your problem. That is like learning second hand. But the way you see things and react to them depends on the instincts and habits you bring to it. Furthermore once you've been round the loop a couple of times you will generate new habits and instincts.

Both first and second hand learning have their disadvantages. Learning things first hand allows you to tailor your learning exactly to what has occurred but it is often slow or dangerous. Imagine trying to learn about snake bites, first hand. And anyway, life is not always moving fast enough or necessarily providing all the information for you to experience all implications of a single action (e.g. global warming). With second hand learning the real dangers are that the situation may have been diagnosed wrongly and therefore the advice offered is not appropriate.

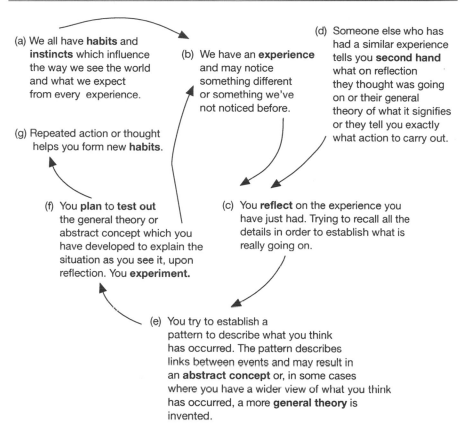

(a) We all have **habits** and **instincts** which influence the way we see the world and what we expect from every experience.

(b) We have an **experience** and may notice something different or something we've not noticed before.

(d) Someone else who has had a similar experience tells you **second hand** what on reflection they thought was going on or their general theory of what it signifies or they tell you exactly what action to carry out.

(g) Repeated action or thought helps you form new **habits**.

(f) You **plan** to **test out** the general theory or abstract concept which you have developed to explain the situation as you **see** it, upon reflection. You **experiment.**

(c) You **reflect** on the experience you have just had. Trying to recall all the details in order to establish what is really going on.

(e) You try to establish a pattern to describe what you think has occurred. The pattern describes links between events and may result in an **abstract concept** or, in some cases where you have a wider view of what you think has occurred, a more **general theory** is invented.

Fig.2.2 The Learning Cycle, Part 1 – The Theory

If it is obviously wrong you may reject it either when you think about it or when you try to look for the general rules which it suggests or at the planning stage.

Most project leaders are deficient in one or more areas of the cycle. They do not smoothly work their way around it. The most common pattern I have seen, is that they jump backwards and forwards from an experience to a general theory and back again. You may have seen this pattern yourself. There is a problem. The project leader leaps in, gathers the immediately available facts, jumps to a conclusion, issues orders and gets to work. It doesn't really solve the problem, only the immediate symptoms. In no time the problem reappears, often in a slightly different guise and has to be 'sorted out' again. I call this the Batman Trap. Batman and Robin never stop to ask themselves why Gotham City is so full of 'baddies' and crooks. Nor do they look for long term solutions to the high crime rate. They simply

117

bash and biff the 'baddies' and then wait for the bat phone to ring again so that they can leap into the bat mobile and drive off to find the next crook so that they can bash and biff him too!

In general, project leaders, rather than learning from their experiences simply learn their experiences. Think of project leaders you know. How often, when confronted with new situations, have they simply ended up recounting to you the full narrative history of the Whizzgo-disgo project of 1945? At the end they point out how different things were then or how much they are the same now. Apparently, they have failed to go through the third step of the cycle and do not have any generalised theories or concepts which they can easily apply to new situations.

What makes learning even more difficult is the fact that the more successful you have been in the past, the more you are hindered by past habits you have built up.

The first time I got into a glider I experienced similar sensations to those I had had on my first driving lesson. There were many similarities. For a start I had to ease myself into the seat, taking care not to put my foot through the canvas fuselage. Knobs and dials stared me squarely in the face: there was even a speedometer! As I squared up to face them my instructor told me to 'Adjust the seat so that it is comfortable.' I naturally assumed that it was going to be like driving a car. A car, modified for the lack of space, so that instead of having a steering wheel it had a joy-stick. The main controls were again pointed out in the usual meaningless fashion. I had no idea how they would actually interact once airborne.

The tow plane drew up in front of us and revved its engines. Once connected, it dragged us up to two thousand feet and left us there in silence, gliding in a straight line travelling north west. It was a marvellous sensation. The rush of air, the toy-like size of houses and farms on the ground. It was bliss. And then the instructor said to me, 'You have control. I would like you to turn to the right.'

'No sweat.' I thought, as I tightened my grip on the joystick and swung it right. Nothing happened. I moved it further and then all of a sudden the right wing began to drop very fast. I could see the ground directly below. It was a sickening sensation but what was worse was that I could see that we were still travelling north west. I pulled the joystick back into the middle but the wing stayed down! Furthermore, the glider had started to speed up. I could hear the wind rushing by faster and faster. By now I was totally confused and starting to panic. Instinctively, I tried to slow down by pushing my right foot down hard on the brake. Only it wasn't a brake, it was the pedal that controlled the rudder. I felt my stomach churn as the tail end of the glider swung out violently to the left. We skidded along. But we were still travelling north west. I was determined not to let on that I was in difficulties and as calmly as I could manage, asked the instructor to take back control.

My instincts were all wrong. To turn a car you only do one thing, you move the steering wheel. The car responds immediately. You can correct your turn by turning the wheel to match the curve. To return the car to the straight and narrow you turn the wheel back to the central position. If you wish to slow down or stop you simply press on the brake. The harder you press the quicker it stops. Cars only travel along sideways when you skid them on a slippery surface.

To turn a glider you do two things, you move the joystick and the rudder together. There is a time lag, and then the glider responds. It banks at a continuously increasing angle until you return the stick to the central position and straighten up the rudder. To level out you have to repeat the process in reverse. Putting the joystick in the central position simply says to the glider, 'don't change your angle of banking'. If you wish to slow down you pull the joystick backwards. This pulls up the nose as the plane tries to climb. If you pull too hard however the glider stalls and falls from the sky. Gliders always travel sideways if you fail to co-ordinate the movement of the stick and rudder.

The real barrier is that my habits in the car were so deeply ingrained I kept **doing** things wrong long after I **knew** the correct thing to do. My real learning point was that the similarities which I had noticed at the start of the flight had turned all my sensors off. I was so firmly convinced in my habitual thinking that the experience I was going to go through was exactly the same as driving a car that I could not interpret what was happening accurately. Eventually the instructor had to explain it to me. The problem with instincts and habits is that they stop you from seeing what is actually there.

I didn't have much success with second hand learning either. On my second trip my instructor explained to me how to ensure that once airborne the glider's natural descent is at a rate which produces the best gliding period. This is done by setting an adjustment on part of the wing flaps so that they create the correct angle for lift when the joystick is central. The process is known as 'setting the trim' or 'trimming the wings'.

Pointing to the cable which was used for this he said, 'I find, that if I line up the green mark with the second notch, it sails liked a dream.' I think that he was right. Right for the case where the glider pilot is five foot two and weighs ten stone. I am five foot seven and weigh fifteen stone. I took his advice on my next trip. It was a very short trip. One that I hardly remember at all. The glider sank like a stone.

DO YOU HAVE A LEARNING DEFICIENCY?

Instinct and habit

Do you actively try to seek out what is different in every situation you meet to make sure that you are seeing 'What is really there' and not just 'What you expect to see'?

Get into the habit of asking yourself 'What am I missing?' 'Is there something that I haven't noticed?'

Second hand learning

How much of your time do you spend actively searching for second hand learning?

Do you actively screen your second hand learning?

- reflect on it to check that it rings true?
- check that the general theory makes sense in your case and fits the facts?
- plan and carry out a few experiments to check its validity?

First hand learning

Go back to the questionnaire you completed at the start of this section. To score it work **down column by column** for the four columns. Do not add up up the scores in each column. Below the *specific rows* which relate to correctly scoring the questionnaire are listed.

The ability to fully absorb *experiences* you meet with.
   Add your scores in the first column for rows 2 + 3 + 4 + 5 + 7 + 8

_____

The ability to fully *reflect* upon your experiences.
   Add your scores in the second column for rows 1 + 3 + 6 + 7 + 8 + 9

_____

The ability to build *general theories* from your conclusions.
   Add your scores in the third column for rows 2 + 3 + 4 + 5 + 8 + 9

_____

The ability to *plan* your way to *experiment* to test out your theory.
   Add your scores in the fourth column for rows 1 + 3 + 6 + 7 + 8 + 9

_____

In my experience a score of less than ten suggests that you do not do that step of the cycle very well. Any imbalance (a range of more than five) also suggests that you may have some difficulty with the cycle. The key to effective learning is being competent in each step when appropriate.

To manage in a changing environment, you must become interested, no, **obsessed** by what you are learning. Projects by their nature are 'one-offs'. Furthermore as they evolve the demands made on you and the other stakeholders change. In the early stages you need to learn what each stakeholder thinks success is. However, as you go on and they get a greater understanding of what can actually be delivered by the project, their view of successful change will alter and you will need to re-learn this.

Also, as it evolves, you may need to invent roles and methods of working and reporting progress. These will also change as the needs of the project change. It is pointless to continue reporting on the completion of the design once the user testing has been started. But human beings are slow to throw out things they have developed. Reporting soon becomes a habit. What this means is that people can continue to demand ways of working to be perpetuated long after they stop being essential to the running of the project. It seems as if the project, that is the team and all its stakeholders, can form habits in almost the same way as you do.

In fact organisations can and **do** learn, and project teams, as a subset of these, also learn. I believe that, contrary to the current vogue which says that organisations need to begin to learn, that they already do so with great speed and efficiency. They may not actually get it right all the time but one thing which they are excellent at is forming habits. Habits are things which people in the organisation do instinctively. Since they are formed haphazardly they may often be conflicting, and since they persist long after the situation which led to the learning has passed, they are usually inappropriate and unhelpful. The sum total of all the organisational habits which have been acquired is sometimes referred to as the organisational culture.

There is a very special characteristic to organisational learning which it is essential for you to understand if you wish to manage change in chunks. When organisations learn, the learning is split up between all the members of the organisation, each one having to learn a small part of the whole, the part that relates specifically to them (steps e and f in the cycle above). The learning is thus very effective, like ants in an anthill, and habits are shared between them. What this means is that to break an organisational habit you will need to gain access to all, or at least many, of the stakeholders involved. This is particularly important for project leaders managing internal or change projects.

121

INDIVIDUAL TAILORING

Fog and Quest projects: *As project leader you will need to make sure that you go round the loop. The degree and speed of learning is a critical factor in determining whether or not the project succeeds*

Change or Joint venture projects: *As you learn you will need to ensure that the rest of the organisation learns (see Stakeholder mapping 2.2.1) and unlearns what it thought it previously knew. Typically, part of the project will involve tasks whose sole purpose is to disconfirm or eliminate previously held conceptions which no longer fit in with current understanding. Bubble diagrams (Section 2.1.1 Blowing Bubbles) can be a very useful method of doing this.*

Section 2.1.1
Blowing Bubbles

Thinking is that waste of time between seeing something and knowing what to do about it . . .
Edward de Bono

(Aside: In Chapter Two you may have been wondering what the circles and arrows which Franck drew on the napkin meant. And you may have been slightly frustrated by Franck's answer that he was 'blowing bubbles'.)

Blowing bubbles is the most effective method I know for getting you rapidly round *all* the aspects of the learning process. It challenges habits in thinking by forcing you to justify your conclusions and makes you notice what is actually happening in the experience you have gone through. It encourages second hand inputs into your learning but insists that you check them thoroughly to make sure that they are appropriate and correct. Finally, it guides you systematically round the loop of reflection, to a general theory and clearly to what actions you must plan in order to solve the problems you face.

One of the key things that having learnt something allows you to do is to recognise patterns. Try this:

If the sun sinks below the horizon **then** ....

and if it is a clear sky **then** ....

So there you go! You can, after all, predict the future! But not very far into the future, because other factors come into play. For example, in winter the pattern may be different or a storm may come up suddenly. The moon may be full and unexpectedly bright. However, we can use the same method to **predict** the past: largely because if we have lived through or observed the past or current events, we will have a fuller picture which includes most of all the expected and unexpected factors. And with a little testing and research *we can find out about things which have occurred* even if *we did not observe them ourselves first hand.* I use the word **predict** deliberately. Have you noticed how, at work, sometimes you solve a problem? It goes away for a short time and then it pops up again? Sometimes the same, sometimes in a different guise? It's as if you are 'fire fighting'. So despite your tremendous effort, no sooner have you damped down the flames at the top of the inferno than they are re-lit by the hot ashes underneath. You

123

never quite get the water to the ashes underneath. After all, who has time to think when there is a fire raging?

Blowing bubbles is a method for working out exactly what in the past or in current events, is causing the problems you are trying to overcome. The idea is that once you find what the real underlying problem is and fix it, it will stay fixed. Of course some people prefer fighting fires to solving the underlying problem. (Aside: If you are one of those people, this method holds nothing for you. You probably didn't enjoy reading the narrative discussions in the first part of the book.)

The method forces you round the learning cycle. The current and past provide the experience to blow a bubble. You must reflect and build a general theory which you then test out. Your test involves using things you have observed first or second hand in the current or past.

A SIMPLE EXAMPLE

When I was a student in London I couldn't afford to live in the centre. So instead, I lived some way out and bought myself an old banger to get to and from college. We had a number of lecturers who were more interested in whether you were on time for lectures than whether you actually learnt anything. There was a problem which I often met in trying to meet their goals. See if you can help me solve it.

> It's a quarter to nine. Lectures start at nine and you've overslept. You reach for the chair where your jeans and favourite jumper lie in a crumpled mess and try to put them on whilst moving between the bedroom and the bathroom. You grab your case and hurtle down the stairs to your bashed up old 1969 Mk1 (near white, with rust spots) Ford Escort. You leap in, turn the key in the ignition, the engine turns over but won't start. You don't want to be late. You definitely do not want to walk the four miles to college and buses are infrequent and take a long tortuous route. No choice but to get it to start.
>
> Is the battery flat? You turn on the radio and the Radio One jingle blares out at you. The battery is not completely flat. But just to be sure that it's not the battery you turn on the lights and get out to check if they are dim. They are not. Once you clean the glass they are very bright indeed. So you know that it's not the battery.

You could write down the way you figure it out like this:

My car won't start!
Why?
Maybe the battery is flat.
But if the battery was flat the radio would not come on.

It does.
If the battery was flat the lights should be dim.
The lights are very bright.
So it probably isn't being caused by a flat battery.

Or like this:

THERE IS A PROBLEM:	My car won't start!
I NEED TO FIND OUT HOW IT HAS ARISEN:	Why?
I GUESS AT A CAUSE:	Maybe the battery is flat?
I KNOW THAT ANY CAUSE WILL BRING ABOUT SEVERAL OTHER EFFECTS, GOOD OR BAD:	But if the battery was flat the radio would not come on.
I LOOK FOR ANYTHING WHICH I SHOULD EXPECT TO SEE IF MY GUESSED CAUSE IS PRESENT, THINGS I WOULD BE UNLIKELY TO SEE IF THE CAUSE IS ABSENT:	
I CHECK TO SEE IF THE EFFECTS ARE PRESENT OR ABSENT:	It does.
I CONTINUE TO LOOK FOR ANYTHING THAT I SHOULD EXPECT TO SEE IF MY GUESSED CAUSE IS PRESENT, THINGS I WOULD BE UNLIKELY TO SEE IF THE CAUSE IS ABSENT:	If the battery was flat the lights should be dim.
I CHECK TO SEE IF THE EFFECTS ARE PRESENT OR ABSENT:	The lights are very bright.
I REPEAT THE LAST TWO STEPS UNTIL I AM CONVINCED THAT I HAVE EITHER FOUND EVIDENCE WHICH SUGGESTS THAT I WAS PROBABLY RIGHT WITH MY INITIAL GUESS OR FOUND THAT MY EVIDENCE DOES NOT FIT WITH MY GUESS AT THE CAUSE:	
I THEN CONCLUDE THAT THE GUESS IS EITHER CORRECT OR WRONG:	So it probably isn't being caused by the battery being flat.

Or in terms of bubbles you would draw:

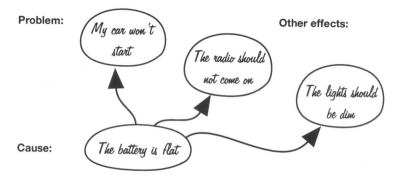

Fig. 2.3 Blowing bubbles – first guess

The direction of the arrows, as you will see later, is very important. The problem or effect you are trying to understand should be at the arrow head. Your guess of the cause goes at the base of the arrow. Try to draw them from the top of a bubble (base of arrow) to the bottom (tip of arrow) **every** time.

When you follow an arrow from tip to base you are asking '**Why**?'

WHY?

When you follow an arrow from base to tip you are predicting that '**If**' the cause is correct '**Then**' certain other effects will be expected.

IF . . .   THEN . . .
⟶

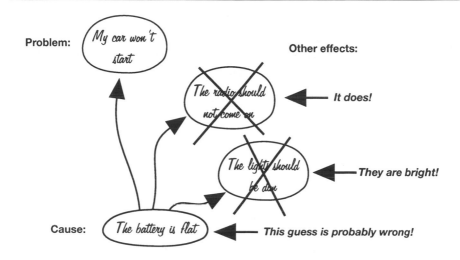

Fig. 2.4 Blowing bubbles – first guess invalidated

The bubbles are crossed out because, in reality, I did not see any of the effects which were predicted by my guess.

You're back to square one. You need to try again. You could have run out of petrol. You glance at the gauge and then remember that it hasn't worked since the last time you serviced the car yourself. You rock the car from side to side and listen to hear the petrol sloshing about. You can't hear anything but then it's noisy so close to the main road. So you get the petrol can out instead and pour about a gallon in and try again. You still have no luck. The engine turns over with a woeful whine.

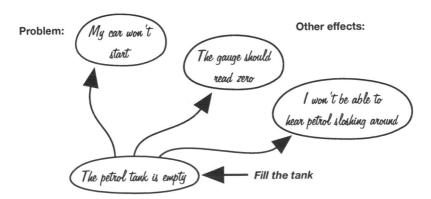

Fig. 2.5 Blowing bubbles – second guess

Sometimes it is not possible to immediately check whether the effects you expect to see are present. You may need to go off and do some further research. Here you have decided instead to assume that your guess is right and to 'fire fight'. You do this by carrying out an action which is the opposite of whatever is written in the bubble. So 'the tank is empty' becomes 'fill the tank'.

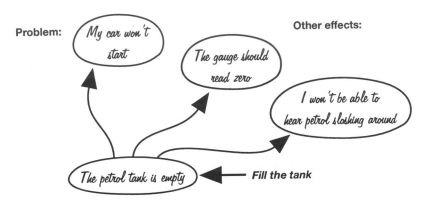

Fig. 2.6 Blowing bubbles – second guess solved

By now you are getting desperate. It is five to nine. You think 'Maybe there isn't any electrical power reaching the spark plugs.' You rapidly unscrew one and hold it against the engine block. You are a bit wary of this procedure. The last time you did this you gave yourself a powerful and nasty shock. You reach in through the window and turn the key. The engine turns over but you do not see a spark. 'Got it!' you think. But although you know the cause, you now need to find out why no power is reaching the plugs. That is, 'What is causing the first cause?'

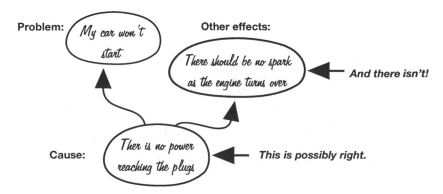

Fig 2.7 Blowing bubbles – third guess validated

You think to yourself, 'Perhaps the connections are loose.' You try to jiggle the leads from side to side to see if they move. They don't.

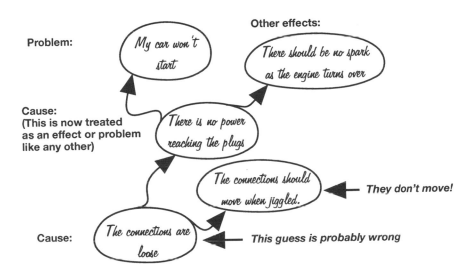

Fig 2.8 Blowing bubbles – fourth guess invalidated

Again, if we looked at your thoughts they would look like this:

THERE IS A STILL A PROBLEM:	Because there is no electrical power to the plugs my car won't start!
I NEED TO FIND OUT HOW IT HAS ARISEN:	Why?
I GUESS AT A CAUSE:	Perhaps the connections are loose?
I KNOW THAT ANY CAUSE WILL CAUSE SEVERAL OTHER EFFECTS, GOOD OR BAD:	But if the connections were loose they would move when jiggled.

This part gets a bit circular and boring.

The only other reason you can think of which would explain the lack of power to the plugs is that the distributor is wet and shorting out. You ease the distributor cap off and run your finger round inside it. It feels damp. You take your handkerchief out and thoroughly wipe all the metal surfaces to dry them.

129

You glance at your watch. It looks as if, if you leave now and drive like a mad person, you may just make it. You slide in behind the wheel, utter a silent prayer and turn the key. After coughing twice the engine stutters to life.

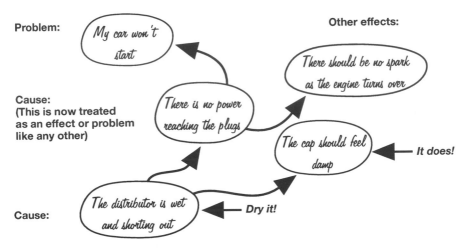

Fig. 2.9 Blowing bubbles – fifth guess validated

You know that you have successfully fought this fire. If you want to put the fire out for good, you will need to find the **underlying or root cause** and fix it, then the problem should stay fixed. You know that you should find out why the distributor is wet. You will need to keep asking 'why?' until you come to a cause which is completely out of your control. At this point you have gone as far as you can. Fix *this* cause and the problem goes away for you.

Can you see from this simplistic example how the process works? It's pure logic. In first hand learning terms, first you have the experience, then you reflect on what actually happened by blowing bubbles. At the end of the process you will have established both the underlying root cause and a full and complete theory explaining how the problem arose in the first place. You then work out how to remove the root cause and the specific problem you are dealing with goes away.

A MORE COMPLEX PROBLEM

Real-life business problems are a lot more complex. For a start they are less mechanical and require far more imagination in developing guesses. And anyway, many problems relate to human behaviour or thought inter-mingled with organisational measures, policies, and reward and punish-ment systems. And even worse, you usually find that each problem or effect has more than one cause!

Can you still create a meaningful bubble diagram? The answer is yes. But it takes longer and it takes a lot more care. For a start each bubble must be written as a full sentence. For example, 'Battery' as an explanation for the car not starting is not really clear enough. Instead you must write 'The battery is flat.' Use names wherever possible or 'our' or 'we'. You must be especially careful at the step where you check the expected effects of your guess. You need to check both for effects you would expect and check for effects which would never occur if the guess is in place. For example, if the problem is 'we have built large amounts of finished goods which we can't sell.' And we ask 'Why?' The answer may be that, 'Our staff are paid a large bonus for production quantity.' The things you would expect to see around you if you worked in this factory would be people putting a lot of effort into completing jobs just before the output is counted. So if output is measured daily you will see that 'the last hour of the day is devoted to finishing off as many jobs as possible'. You will not see 'people giving up vast amounts of time to quality or product improvement', unless they can see how this would 'speed up the production rate'.

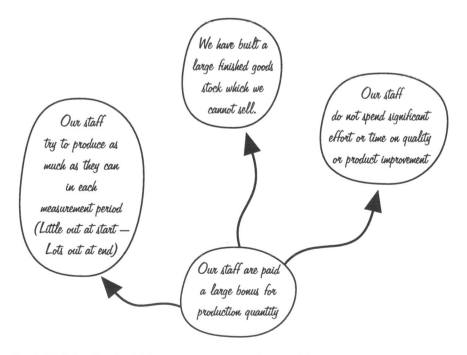

Fig 2.10 Blowing bubbles – a more complex problem

It is a lot harder to learn to build a bubble diagram from written instructions than from a taught dialogue but I will give it my best shot. I will put sketches of **roughly** how your bubble diagram should look at each stage.

WORKING OUT WHAT CHUNKS TO CHANGE BY BUILDING A BUBBLE DIAGRAM

STEP 1 GET THREE SHEETS OF A3 PAPER

STEP 2 ON THE FIRST SHEET WRITE DOWN (AS SENTENCES) THE MAJOR BUSINESS PROBLEMS WHICH CONCERN YOU.

STEP 3 CHOOSE 3 OR 4 WHICH ARE SUITABLY DIFFERENT OR SEEM UNRELATED.

STEP 4 PLACE YOUR SECOND SHEET LANDSCAPE AND WRITE OUT THE PROBLEMS, IN BUBBLES, STARTING ABOUT A THIRD OF THE WAY DOWN.

STEP 5 START WITH THE PROBLEM YOU FEEL MOST CONFIDENT THAT YOU UNDERSTAND. GUESS A CAUSE AND CHECK THE EFFECTS. KEEP CHECKING UNTIL YOU ARE SATISFIED THAT YOUR GUESS IS EITHER RIGHT OR WRONG.

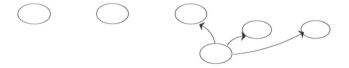

STEP 6 STAY WITH THE SAME BUBBLE. DO NOT MOVE ONTO ANOTHER ONE YET. REPEAT STEP 5 UNTIL YOU HAVE RUN OUT OF GUESSES FOR THAT SINGLE PROBLEM.

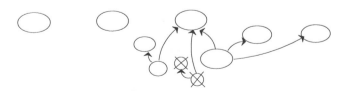

STEP 7 GO TO THE NEXT PROBLEM AND REPEAT STEPS 5 AND 6. YOU MAY FIND THAT SOME OF THE GUESSES OR EFFECTS YOU HAVE WRITTEN DOWN

ARE GUESSES OR EFFECTS WHICH YOU NEED AS YOU WORK ON THIS SECOND PROBLEM. IF YOU FIND THAT THIS IS THE CASE DON'T DUPLICATE WHAT YOU HAVE ALREADY WRITTEN, SIMPLY JOIN UP THE BUBBLES WITH ARROWS (**IF** ⟶ **THEN** or **WHY?** ⟵ **BECAUSE**).

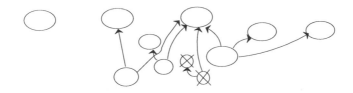

STEP 8 REPEAT STEP 7 FOR THE REMAINING 1 OR 2 PROBLEMS.

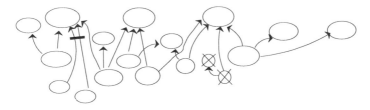

STEP 9 READ WHAT YOU HAVE WRITTEN DOWN AND SEE IF YOU CAN ADD ANY MORE ARROWS. TRY TO LINK TO THE PROBLEMS YOU STARTED WITH. (IF YOU NEED AN 'AND' RECORD THIS WITH A HORIZONTAL BAR ACROSS TWO ARROWS.)

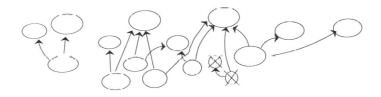

STEP 10 CHECK TO SEE IF YOU CAN TRACE, WITHOUT LIFTING YOUR PENCIL OFF THE PAGE, A LINE WHICH GOES UP OR DOWN ARROWS AND PASSES THROUGH ALL THE PROBLEMS YOU STARTED WITH. IF YOU CAN, SKIP TO STEP 12

STEP 11 LOOK FOR BUBBLES WHICH DON'T HAVE ANY ARROWS GOING TO THEM. FOR EACH ONE OF THESE BUBBLES GO BACK TO STEP 5.

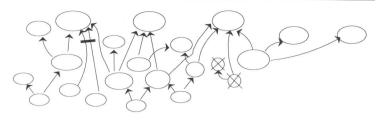

STEP 12 GO BACK TO YOUR FIRST SHEET AND READ THROUGH YOUR LIST OF PROBLEMS. YOU WILL SEE THAT ON YOUR BUBBLE DIAGRAM YOU HAVE WRITTEN DOWN THEIR CAUSES. FILL IN THE TOP THIRD OF YOUR SECOND SHEET WITH BUBBLES OF THE REMAINING PROBLEMS. (IN THE VERY UNLIKELY EVENT THAT YOU CANNOT DIRECTLY TRANSFER ONE OR TWO OF YOUR LIST OF PROBLEMS DIRECTLY ONTO THE BUBBLE CHART, WRITE THEM IN THE TOP THIRD AND GO BACK TO STEP 5).

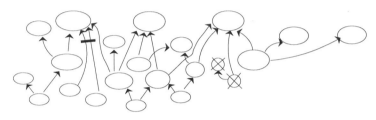

STEP 13 YOU NOW NEED TO FILL IN THE TOP OF THE SECOND SHEET. FOR EACH OF YOUR ORIGINAL PROBLEMS COMPLETE THE SENTENCE IF {ORIGINAL PROBLEM} THEN ... {NEW BUBBLE TO BE DRAWN IN ABOVE THE ORIGINAL PROBLEM BUBBLE}. NOW YOUR BUBBLE CHART SHOULD ALSO HAVE SOME OF THE PROBLEMS YOU FEEL YOU HAVE BUT DID NOT INCLUDE ON YOUR ORIGINAL LIST BECAUSE YOU FELT THAT THEY WERE LESS WEIGHTY!

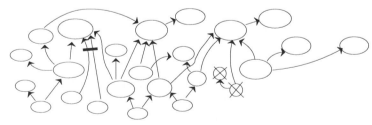

STEP 14 LOOK FOR THE REMAINING BUBBLES WHICH DO NOT HAVE AN ARROW GOING TO THEM. CHOOSE ONE AND GUESS A CAUSE AND CHECK THE EFFECTS. KEEP CHECKING UNTIL YOU ARE SATISFIED THAT YOUR GUESS IS EITHER RIGHT OR WRONG. STAY WITH THE SAME BUBBLE. DO NOT MOVE ONTO ANOTHER ONE YET UNTIL YOU HAVE RUN OUT OF GUESSES FOR THAT SINGLE PROBLEM.

STEP 15 REPEAT STEP 14 UNTIL YOU COME ACROSS BUBBLES WHICH ARE
CLEARLY OUT OF YOUR CONTROL AND INFLUENCE;
    'The government have just passed new legislation'
    'Competitors have just launched a new product'
OR THE **CAUSE IS HISTORIC:**;
    'We were taken over in 1978'
OR **THE RESULT OF A POLICY**;
    'We pay people by the hour'
    'Our staff are paid a large bonus for production quantity'
OR IT MAY SIMPLY BE A **PHYSICAL REALITY** SUCH AS;
    'We just haven't got enough of the right type of staff
    'Our equipment can not manufacture any faster'

These bubbles will explain the underlying causes. It is unusual to have more than half a dozen, so if you have more you may be doing something wrong. Usually it is because you have tried to force the process to come up with your pet theory and your checks on effects have not been rigorous. Never mind, step 16 should sort you out.

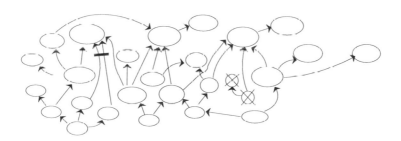

STEP 16 YOU ARE GOING TO READ YOUR BUBBLE CHART BACK TO YOURSELF,
OUT LOUD TO CHECK THAT YOU HAVEN'T GONE WRONG ANYWHERE.
START AT THE BOTTOM AND FOLLOW THE ARROWS UPWARDS.

A QUICK TEST

Try this example.

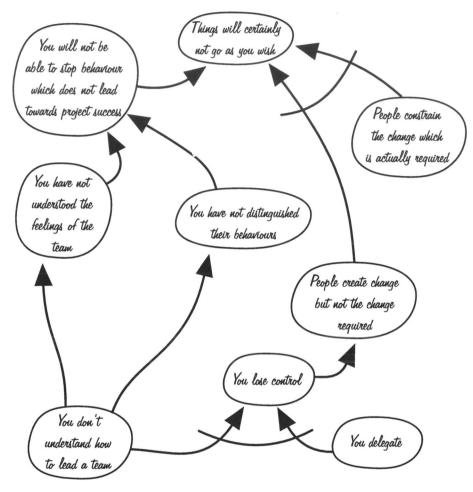

Fig 2.11

Solution

'**If** you don't understand how to lead a team, **And If** you delegate, **Then** things certainly would not go as you wished.

It would happen like this. First, what would happen would be that you would lose control. Since you've lost control *people will create change* but not the change required. Now, they will also *constrain change*, and knowing Murphy's law it is bound to be precisely the change which is actually required.'

'If you didn't know how to lead a team then when, quite naturally, the project starts to go astray you will not have understood the feelings of the team and you will not have distinguished their behaviours, and so you will not be able to stop behaviour which did not lead towards project success. If you can't stop behaviour which does not lead to project success then things will certainly not go as you wish.'

Section 2.1.2
Managing Review

Today's Problems come from Yesterday's solutions
Peter M. Senge

What is the purpose of review? Yes, I know you feel that is it is important to have reviews. However, in most projects, reviews are infrequent and often ineffectual. If you seriously want to review progress in the project and learn as you go along or learn for next time, you will need to make sure that you plan reviews into your time schedule and wherever possible make them coincide with time buffers (See Section 2.3.2 Pacing Yourself). I believe that the purpose of review is to provide a formal opportunity for the project leader and all the stakeholders to learn; to reflect on what has happened so far in the projects. Was it expected? Unexpected? To establish what the implications are for each of them and for the project overall and to establish what actions need to be taken to amend or remedy the situation.

The best method I know for carrying out review I call **Action Replay**. I invented this method after several managers told me that they couldn't do reviews because they couldn't remember anything which happened more than a day earlier. The review is very structured but actually carried out *backwards*.

A friend of mine was once asked by his organisation to put together a management development programme for his company. He had developed a programme using a range of tutors. The programme had run but had not been received well by the participants and had come in far over budget. He asked me in to help with the review. I was to meet the team in a hotel off the motorway. I turned up and walked into a room of the most depressed people I had seen in a long time. 'Why are you so glum?' I asked.

'We have screwed it up and we don't know why,' came the mumbled answer.

'What happened yesterday?'

'Yesterday we finally worked through the course reviews and discovered that they were terrible.'

'How did they get to be terrible without you noticing?'

'Well they didn't give us the feedback till the end.'

'Who decided that they shouldn't give you feedback until the end?'

There was a short silence. 'I guess we all did,' they replied.

'Where did it all start to go wrong?'

'I guess it was when we forgot to tell them that they should tell us about the course as we went along.'

'Why did you forget?'

'We hadn't written it into our briefing notes. I guess we should make a note of it for next time.'

'OK, what happened the day before yesterday?' . . .

ACTION REPLAY™

STEP 1   ASK **WHEN** WE STARTED/FINISHED THE PERIOD UNDER REVIEW?
           DECIDE THE TIME PERIOD THAT THE REVIEW IS TO COVER.

STEP 2   ASK **WHAT** WE HAVE DONE? START WITH THE MOST RECENT
           MEMORIES.
           FOR EXAMPLE, 'WHAT WENT RIGHT/WRONG YESTERDAY?'

STEP 3   ASK **HOW** YESTERDAY'S OUTCOMES AROSE? FOR EXAMPLE,
           'HOW DID WE GET IT TO WORK SO WELL?'

STEP 4   ASK **WHO** WAS INVOLVED? THE STAKEHOLDERS WILL HAVE THE
           BEST IDEA OF WHAT ACTUALLY HAPPENED. FOR EXAMPLE,
           'WHO SET IT UP THIS WAY?' BE CAREFUL WITH THIS QUESTION
           THAT YOU ARE NOT APPEARING TO APPORTION BLAME.

STEP 5   ASK **WHERE** IT WENT RIGHT OR WRONG? ESTABLISH THE KEY
           STEPS WHICH GOT US HERE.

STEP 6   ASK **WHY** IT HAPPENED? IF THE ANSWER IS COMPLEX DRAW A
           BUBBLE DIAGRAM.

STEP 7   SUMMARISE WHAT YOU HAVE LEARNED AS A GENERAL PRIN-
           CIPLE AND MAKE SURE THAT ALL THE OTHER REVIEWERS
           UNDERSTAND IT (SEE SECTION 2.3.3 on COMMUNICATING OUT).

STEP 8   MAKE SURE THAT ANY ACTIONS ARISING FROM WHAT YOU HAVE
           LEARNT ARE OWNED.

STEP 9   REPEAT STEPS FOR THE PREVIOUS DAY.

Section 2.2
RECOGNISING STAKEHOLDERS

The reality of the world, the complexity of the immediate environment, the need for stakeholder symmetry must not be lost in the colourful glories of the kaleidoscopic vision.
Warren Bennis

'What did we decide we meant by a *successful project*?' Franck demands.

I know that he has got me, so I don't answer, but I know he's right. *Project success is and can only be defined by the stakeholders.*

So who are these stakeholders then? They are people who are affected by your chunk of change. But what is it that affects them? Why do they react? We saw earlier in Chapter Six that the third law of change governs how people react in a changing environment. We still need to know why they react the way that they do. I have a confession to make. Everything in this book is wrong!

No, I joke. But what was your immediate reaction? Was it logical or emotional? My guess is that the first words which went through your mind are unprintable, not to be seen by civilised people. I guess your reaction was emotional. This is completely human. It's the biological fight or flight reaction at work. It goes back to humans at the dawn of civilisation.

You're out doing your hunter-gatherer bit. Walking through the good old primeval forest. There is the steady chirp, chirp of the birds and the moaning of the wind in the trees above. Suddenly there is a loud rustling noise in the bushes behind you. It could be a bird, a mouse, a man-eating sabre toothed tiger. Instantly your body tenses up, the adrenalin starts to flow. Something has *changed*. It could be a threat to your security. I suspect that those of us who are alive now had ancestors who were the more successful at surviving in that rather inhospitable environment. My guess is that my ancestors were the ones who **fled in mindless terror** at the first sign of any *change* and not the ones who **stood around being logical** about it and working out the probabilities of the noise being the sound of a man-eating sabre toothed tiger pushing it's way through the undergrowth. I think that once they were safely away, *then* and only then did they try to work out what the cause of the rustle had been.

In other words their first reaction was emotional and then, after they had got their breath back, logical. ***Confronted with change, people's first reaction is emotional and then if you are lucky they then move into the logical phase***. This argument makes the current vogue, which

141

suggests that we must all learn to love change, look a little bit hollow for a species which has spent hundreds of years trying to survive it. There is probably little chance that we will ever love imposed or surprise change.

If your change surprises your stakeholders you will make them react emotionally: probably with fear. Fear is the most likely emotion.

> You're in a meeting. You have just announced some of the implications of the project. All the other stakeholders at the meeting are silent but one stakeholder reacts and disagrees strongly with you. You turn to the stakeholder to 'put them right'. You need them to get on with the change. You can't afford to have them frightened and uncertain and unable to help you deliver the project, so you reason with them. You take great pains to explain how important the project is to the organisation, how important it is to be progressive in these demanding times. And you stress how important it is for the stakeholder to do such and such. You explain to the others what they are to do to. They all nod and agree and then you leave the meeting. Two weeks later you realise that no one, not one of the stakeholder's has kept their promises.

Do you recognise this? What has happened?

Your 'other half' is upset for some reason and comes to you and says, 'You don't like me.' You reply, 'Yes I do,' and then start to list all the evidence to support this. 'Last Valentine's Day I bought you a dozen red roses. Every time I've been away on business I've called you before bedtime in spite of the cost of hotel phone calls. I remembered your birthday.' Does this work? Definitely not! What works is if you give them a big hug. **You use logic to overcome logic. You use emotion to overcome emotion.** I know you are smiling at this revelation. But there is one small problem. At work you can't go around giving people hugs unsolicited. You get fired for that sort of thing. But you need another emotion. The most common one to use at work, ironically, is fear. We use fear to overcome someone else's fear. What else are we doing when we say to someone, 'You think things are bad now, but if you don't change we may all be out of a job,' or 'It is important for your promotion to demonstrate flexibility to new ways of working.' I've done it and I guess that you have too. You've probably also used greed or desire, 'How much you could get out of this,' or excitement and enthusiasm, 'It's going to be great fun!' But I guess that you've used other emotions as well.

> You're in a meeting and an idea has been tossed into the middle. For the past ten minutes every one, except one person, has been pouring cold water on the idea. In fact that person has been describing the benefits of the idea. Whilst everyone can see downsides that person can only see the upside.

Who is this person? Guess. It's the person who thought up the idea in the first place. Thinking up an idea yourself is like deciding to flee, all on your own. There is change but *if you are creating it yourself you do not constrain it*. So if you wish to avoid people constraining change you have to be careful to give them all the information and direction that they need to create the right change themselves.

There is another mechanism which is very effective for people who are non-stakeholders in your change, people who do not feel that your change is aimed at them. If you make it obvious what your change is and make all the advantages and benefits obvious and visible, people will copy you!

PERSONAL STAKEHOLDER MAP

STAKEHOLDERS	Driver organisation (Client, Other Function, J.V. Partners)	Your organisation (Project)	Deliverer (to you) organisations (Subcontractors, Suppliers, J.V. Partners)
Who wants you:	*sponsor:*	*sponsor:*	
To succeed			
To fail			
Who is betting on you:			
To succeed			
To fail			
Who is supporting you:	*Key contact*	*Core team* *Extended team*	
Visibly		*Invisible team*	
Invisibly			
Whose success:		*Key contact*	
Affects you	*Key contact*		
Do you affect			
Who does your change:	*End user*		
Benefit			
Damage			
Who can your change:			
happen without			
not happen without			

(Bottom of bubble diagram)   *Absolutely critical:* —— *Outcome interest:* o *Interest during:* *

Section 2.2.1
Mapping Stakeholders

The way of war is to know your opponents.
Chiu Ming

So who are these stakeholders? Those people who define project success and define for you the boundaries and organisation of your chunk of change?

Perhaps we should make a list of them and try to understand their motivations and agendas, both hidden and open.

> Think about all the people who you need:
> > as resources
> > to take along

> Think about all the people who your change:
> > is likely to affect

> Think about all the people in the sidelines:
> > watching you

Now go back to your bubble diagram (Section 2.1.2. Blowing Bubbles). Look at the bubbles at the bottom of the bubble diagram – *the core drivers*. The bubbles with **no** arrows going into them. What names are mentioned? Where you have written 'we' or 'they' who are you referring to? The people whose names are closest to the bottom of the bubble diagram will be the stakeholders who will have the greatest influence over your project. Why? Because they will need to alter something that they do or don't do in order for your change to become real and be translated into an improvement. Make sure that you have their names written down and underlined or highlighted. Now work your way up the diagram. Look for any other names you have missed. It's easiest to organise the names and groups as a **grid** or a **map**. But I advise drawing two maps. One for your *personal* use and another which you use *publicly* and stick on the wall.

On the personal map some names may appear in more than one row.

Give yourself about a quarter of an hour to complete it. Leave the map for a while and then return to it about an hour later and have another go.

Highlight any stakeholders you have discovered who you hadn't really spotted before completing the map.

What are the implications of the map which you've drawn? Most people will discover a number of things simply by completing the map.

145

Firstly, *there are **more** stakeholders and more important stakeholders than you initially thought there were.*

Secondly, *there are a number of stakeholders who are **absolutely critical** to success.*

And thirdly, *there are actually a number of interested parties who you thought were stakeholders but will best be managed at a distance, best **kept** out of the action.*

1. You will need to rank your stakeholders in terms of two groups. Those ***absolutely critical*** to both progress and success and those who are not. (Usually the sponsors, end users, core team members, key contacts and any names which show up at the bottom of the bubble diagram fall into the first category.)
    Underline all the names in the first category.

2. Now establish which stakeholders are mainly interested in the ***outcome*** of the project and which are mainly interested in what happens ***during*** the project.
    Circle all the names in the first category.
    Put a star against each name in the second category.
    There will be a group who fall into both categories.

(A short note. People who want you to fail are not necessarily bad people; it's just that they don't see the world the way you do. For example, your actions may be threatening their livelihoods.)

At this point you need to copy the names onto the public map, hide the original map and go out and start to establish what their success criteria are.

INDIVIDUAL TAILORING

Open, Fog and Movie projects: *Repeat drawing the stakeholder map frequently. With an open project, new stakeholders will emerge as you go along. If you remember the fog analogy you need to make progress holding hands, you cannot afford to become separated from them. You will need to map them so that you can keep in frequent communication with them.*

Joint Ventures and CommErcial projects: *You will need to do some homework in order to understand the motivations of the stakeholders in the driver organisation. It is usually worth taking some time to establish and understand the internal power and politics of the organisation.*

MAP OF CHANGE STAKEHOLDERS

Client organisation (who have to live with project outcome)	**Project organisation** (your responsibility)	**Supplier/Subcontractor** (provide you with inputs or are delegated parts of the project)
Sponsor:	Sponsor:	Sponsors:
Day-to day or key contact:	Day-to-day or key contact:	Day-to-day or key contact:
End user:	Core team: Extended team:	Sponsors:
		Day-to-day or key contact
	Invisible team:	Sponsors:
		Day-to-day or key contact

Section 2.2.2
Establishing the Hard and Soft Criteria of Success

('You, Sir are drunk!') 'You madam are ugly, but the difference is, I shall be sober in the morning!'
W. Churchill

Inside every stakeholder there is a human being who is making judgements about what you are doing. Some are concerned with the more tangible and fixed aspects of the change you are managing, whilst others are interested in the less tangible, more transient things with which you are concerned. The way that they decide on whether you have succeeded is by measuring you against standards or criteria.

ESTABLISHING SOFT CRITERIA

These are often quite difficult to establish. For a start, people do not always divulge their soft criteria. They feel it is unprofessional or not business-like to talk about the less tangible aspects of the work. But although people tend to talk about hard criteria what they really value and remember are the soft criteria. It is these which influence the acid test, 'Would you do business with this person again?'

> A brilliant business opportunity comes up and you have to travel to a country you have never visited before. Your secretary books you on the privately owned local airline, 'ExecutAir'. You are to travel business class, at a reasonable cost, to arrive on the day before your meeting. How come when you get back to the office the first thing you do is go in to see your secretary. You stand there twitching and mutter through gritted teeth 'Never, ever, book me on ExecutAir again!!'

What happened? All the tangibles seem to have been met. As I said, buying the **first** time round on the basis of **hard** criteria seemed OK at the time so what are you so upset about? Is it the sheer fear and panic that you felt when the pilot, on welcoming you aboard, leaned towards you and a faint smell of alcohol wafted past you? Is it because the cabin crew were slow, rude and unhelpful? Is it because you had to lug your baggage half a mile across the runway to the plane yourself? Or is it the smell of stale cigar smoke that even now clings to you?

In your non-working life you pay a lot of attention to soft criteria. If you had to choose a plumber to put in a new bathroom at home, of course you would consider qualifications and how much the fee would be, but you would also look for someone who came recommended by a friend or neighbour whose judgement you trust. You would want to be sure that the plumber would not leave a mess or make too much noise and so on. The trick is to transfer this very sensible approach to the workplace; to consider the soft criteria of success in managing change.

GENERAL SOFT CRITERIA

There are a number of soft criteria which I have discovered regularly feature in people's measures of success.

Empathy
Your stakeholders need to feel that you see and feel the world from their point of view.

Reliability
Stakeholders usually need to feel that you will do whatever you say you will.

Fault-freeness
Small errors, even typing mistooks can upset some stakeholders. Don't forget that they are relying on you pretty heavily.

Honesty
Very valuable to stakeholders. They can feel comfortable about the process and don't feel that they have to keep watching their backs.

Fun
Most people like to have a laugh whilst they are working. It adds to the sense of achievement.

Aesthetics
Many stakeholders like to be pleased by the appearance of things in projects. For example, clear colour progress charts tend to go down better than cluttered, untidy, black and white charts.

Political sensitivity
Few, if any, stakeholders enjoy being 'dropped in it'. Say your **PRIERS**. Positions, Responsibilities, self Importance, Empires, Reporting lines and Status.

INDIVIDUAL SOFT CRITERIA

With your key stakeholders, it is also necessary to establish their individual foibles and preferences. Individual soft criteria are governed by the values that the person holds dear. You therefore need to establish their values. I usually recommend having an early meeting in the office of the key stakeholder. Here you can pick up clues about what is important to the person.

Is the office tidy? Organised? Is there paper everywhere? How well does this person manage incoming information? Where is the phone? Is it promi-

149

nent? Is there a notice board? How old are the items on it? Is it going to be more effective to communicate by phone or paper?

Does the desk create a formal barrier across the room separating you or is it against the wall allowing access?

Are there any artefacts in the room? Pictures? Photographs of past triumphs? Trophies? Does this person want to be seen by everyone else as successful?

Is there a white board/ flip chart? Does this person like to communicate? Or is there no visible information?

You will stand a better chance if your behaviour reflects their soft criteria.

The second thing to do is to get them to tell you their life story. Say something like 'You've been here a while' or 'You're new to this' or 'You seem to have made rapid progress through this organisation. How did you get into this job/role?' Most people cannot resist talking about themselves to anyone who seems genuinely and fully interested and will end up telling you their life story. In doing that they will give you clues to their values. All you have to do is pay attention.

A few years ago I did some work with a medium sized printing machine manufacturer. After our first meeting I was promptly sent a written summary of our discussions. I then had to phone them about an item of clarification. Again I promptly received a letter summarising our discussions. This happened again after the next phone call. My next meeting was with the MD. Halfway through the meeting I asked him how long he had been with the company. 'Man and boy,' he replied, '35 years.' And then I asked him how he had risen to MD. 'I started on the shop floor. I was keen and worked hard. One day I had a lucky break. We were a bit short of salesmen so I was asked to visit a local customer and get an order. I went to see the customer and discussed the job in detail but I didn't write down the specifics. I almost lost my job over that because we actually supplied the customer with the wrong specifications . . .'

As I heard this, the word 'BINGO!' went through my brain. I had found out why the organisation was so keen on destroying forests. Obviously, as he had risen through the organisation he had insisted that everyone who worked for him wrote things down. Now that everyone worked for him, the whole organisation wrote everything down.

I had also established some of his values:

- People should be keen
- Hard work is good
- People deserve luck

I made sure that all the hard work I put in was clearly visible and that he was aware of any lucky breaks we had with the project and, in terms of future communication, I always wrote everything down.

GENERAL HARD CRITERIA

You also need to establish the hard criteria. To establish the harder, more measurable and tangible criteria for success, you need to answer, 'Why is this change being carried out?'

If you have developed a bubble diagram (Section 2.1.2. Blowing Bubbles) you may be able to answer this for yourself, but you will need to establish this with your outcome stakeholders.

In a business context, their concern is with the *financial contribution* of the project, its *timeliness in providing competitive advantage* and whether it delivers the *specific technical and business objectives it was set up for*.

Next there is a list of most of the key questions you will need answered in order to establish the hard criteria.

Financial contribution

- How much is the project to cost?
- Are we costing this as real money or internal transfers?
- How much revenue will the project generate?
- Does the project generate money itself or does it rely on further business activities? (Is it a commercial project?)
- Are the sums of money substantial with respect to the whole organisation?
- What is the impact of over or underspending?

Timeliness in providing competitive advantage

- When does the change need to be complete by?
- What happens if it's late? (Is it a 'drop dead' project which can't be even a minute late, like building an Olympic stadium?)
- What happens if it is early?
- Who is expecting to receive what we deliver and when?
- Is there a difference between elapsed time and actual time spent working on the project?

- Is there a window of opportunity?
- Who or what is the window bounded by? Competitors? Legislation? Customers? Technology?
- Will starting the project shorten the window as competitors react? Lengthen the window?

Specific technical and business objectives

- What are the specific technical requirements or specifications which the project must meet?
- How much can we deviate from the specifications?
- What happens if the specifications are not met?
- What objectives are definitely not in the scope of the project?
- What objectives are definitely within the scope of the project?

INDIVIDUAL PROJECT HARD CRITERIA

The next sequence of questions is designed to help you establish the relative importance of the three hard criteria in your own chunk. You need to establish your stakeholders' priorities. What do they see as the most important? Financial outcomes, timeliness or the specification of what is delivered? You will need to work the questions into the conversation somehow.

1. If something unforeseen goes wrong and it looks as if we are going to be late, would you rather (a) that I spent some more money, (b) relaxed aspects of the specifications or (c) just let it get a little late?

2. How about if we discovered that it was difficult to meet the specifications, would you rather that we (d) relaxed aspects of the specifications, (e) that I spent some more money or (f) just let it get a little late?

3. Would you be happy if I overspent in order to (g) exceed the specifications, or (h) bring the project in early?

4. How about if we spent extra (j) time or (k) money in order to exceed the expected specifications.

You will probably discover that our stakeholders don't entirely agree on what is most important in the project.

Mark your stakeholders' names on the two triangles below.

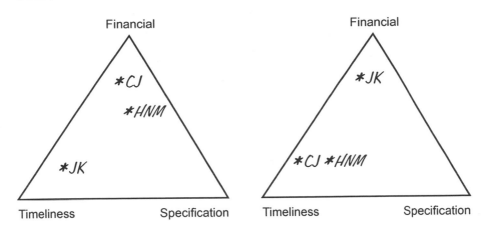

Fig. 2.12 Shareholder's hard criteria – establishing priorities

Are there any disagreements? Now mark your own views on the triangles. Do you agree with your stakeholders? Are you reasonably close? Will they need to be brought closer?

RECORDING SUCCESS CRITERIA

For the project you are working on, what are the success criteria you have identified so far? By now you should have developed an overview, the big picture.

THE BIG PICTURE

Financial contribution

Timeliness in providing competitive advantage

Specific technical and business objectives

General soft criteria to apply overall

Individual soft criteria for key stakeholders

Individual soft criteria for ....

Individual soft criteria for ....

Individual soft criteria for ....

Individual soft criteria for ....

Do your stakeholders agree on the hard and soft criteria? Where are the conflicts? If there are differences of opinion then you *must* negotiate. Don't be a hero. Don't promise the impossible. Don't be a nerd. Don't hope it will all come good. Always negotiate, and negotiate as early as possible.

AGREEING HARD AND SOFT CRITERIA?

What is negotiating? It is definitely **not** an exercise in splitting the difference. Many people think it is. In a change management environment, negotiation takes on a very high profile because it is not acceptable in negotiations for one person to lose and the other to win. If a stakeholder thinks that they have lost, this means to them that the project is not addressing their success criteria and as a result they think it has failed. And it has. Also it is usually the case that at the end of the negotiations, win or lose, you will have to rely on the person you are negotiating with to go away and do further work. It is hard to get commitment and motivation from someone who feels that they have lost the negotiation.

In managing change in chunks, your main focus should be on constructing **win-win** solutions. Win-lose solutions do not assist you in the long term. If you cannot do this, then it is best that, if possible, the stakeholder is eliminated from the project activity.

I don't know about you but I have never met anyone who wakes up in the morning and tells themselves, 'Today I intend to get everything wrong.'

Nobody sets out, intentionally, to get things wrong. Reason, for most people, means their own opinion. This means that *at all costs* in negotiation you must *avoid value laden words* (such as good, best, sensible, insisting or obvious) or any *personal comment* about the person with whom you are negotiating (like slow, stupid, confused or lazy). Avoid saying things like 'Anybody with any sense would see that the most intelligent thing to do is . . .' or 'If you could understand it you would recognise that my solution is the best.' Both of these statements not only insult the person you are talking to, they also make value judgements about the person and the potential outcomes.

Once you understand the different types of conflict you may wish to get on with negotiating. Never rush negotiations. Approach them slowly. Remember the Third Law of Change and why it occurs. You may want to carry out your negotiation in small chunks, one step at a time.

TYPES OF CONFLICT

There are two types of conflict, direct and indirect.

> On a holiday trip to Nairobi I was very much taken by a wooden carving of a giraffe. I asked the price from the vendor and discovered that it was a lot more than I had anticipated. I pulled a face and offered the vendor two thirds of the price which was actually what I could afford. The vendor looked at me in disgust at my suggestion and replied that the offer was unacceptable.

Direct conflict occurs when it appears that one person's success is the exact opposite of the other person's success. The example above illustrates this. In some sales deals, if the seller receives a higher price, the buyer is forced into paying more money. It looks as if the only way it can be settled is by one person winning and the other losing.

> I remember once going into a travel agent's to book myself a canal boat holiday. Seated at the desk next to me a couple seemed to be locked in mortal combat. They were fighting over when and how they were going to get to and from their holiday. They both seemed to be talking at once. 'I think that we should go in the summer, not the autumn like last year.' The man was staring at a page of his filofax saying, 'The latest I can make it is the 5th of July.' 'It must be in the summer or else it starts to get cold.' 'I'm going to be exhausted, so we must travel there and back in comfort.' 'I think that we should fly. Don't you?' 'How much will that cost?'

Indirect conflict occurs when the two people are seeking different but not opposite outcomes. For example, 'I want it this summer' versus 'I want it by the 5th of July'. Or 'I think we should travel to/ from our holiday in comfort' versus 'I think that we should fly to our holiday'.

Indirect conflict

This type of conflict is best resolved by considering subsets. There is usually an area of overlap between different demands which are being voiced.

STEP 1   FIND AN AREA OF AGREEMENT, HOWEVER SMALL.
(IT MAY EVEN BE SOMETHING AS SIMPLE AS THE FACT THAT THEY ARE FINDING IT HARD TO COME TO A CONCLUSION. IN THAT CASE GET THEM TO AGREE ON WHICH PART OF THE ISSUE THEY ARE FINDING IT HARDEST TO AGREE ON.)

STEP 2   CHECK THAT THE PARTIES INVOLVED AGREE THAT THEY AGREE ON THIS AREA.

STEP 3   HIGHLIGHT THE AREAS OF DISAGREEMENT.

STEP 4   SUGGEST THAT THE AREAS OF DISAGREEMENT ARE ADDRESSED ONE AT A TIME.

STEP 5   GET THE PARTIES TO AGREE THAT THE AREAS OF DISAGREEMENT MUST BE ADDRESSED ONE AT A TIME.

STEP 6   CHOOSE THE SIMPLEST AREA OF DISAGREEMENT. DESCRIBE FROM YOUR OWN PERSONAL POINT OF VIEW WHAT YOU THINK EACH PARTY IS SAYING.

STEP 7   THEN DESCRIBE THE SCENARIO IN WHICH ALL THEIR NEEDS ARE MET.

STEP 8   THIS SHOULD MOVE THEM FORWARD ONE STEP. IF IT DOESN'T END THE DISAGREEMENT GO BACK TO THE FIRST STEP.

Let's assume that you are the travel agent dealing with the couple I described earlier. The couple have now been sitting opposite you having a private but public argument for the past half hour. Your patience is wearing thin. You decide to try to negotiate with them. From what you have heard it seems like a case of indirect conflict.

STEP 1   FIND AN AREA OF AGREEMENT HOWEVER SMALL.
(IT MAY EVEN BE SOMETHING AS SIMPLE AS THE FACT THAT THEY ARE FINDING IT HARD TO COME TO A CONCLUSION. IN THAT CASE GET THEM TO AGREE ON WHICH PART OF THE ISSUE THEY ARE FINDING IT HARDEST TO AGREE ON.)

'Excuse me. I couldn't help overhearing, but it seems as if both of you are really looking forward to going on holiday.'

STEP 2　CHECK THAT THE PARTIES INVOLVED AGREE THAT THEY AGREE ON THIS AREA.

'Is this right?' Wait until they have both nodded or said something affirmative.

STEP 3　HIGHLIGHT THE AREAS OF DISAGREEMENT.

'But it seems to me that you are having some difficulty agreeing on when to go and how you might get there.'

STEP 4　SUGGEST THAT THE AREAS OF DISAGREEMENT ARE ADDRESSED ONE AT A TIME.

'Perhaps you could look at the areas of disagreement one at a time. We might find that easier to handle?'

STEP 5　GET THE PARTIES TO AGREE THAT THE AREAS OF DISAGREEMENT MUST BE ADDRESSED ONE AT A TIME.

'What do you think?' Wait for them to nod or say something affirmative.

STEP 6　CHOOSE THE SIMPLEST AREA OF DISAGREEMENT. DESCRIBE FROM YOUR OWN PERSONAL POINT OF VIEW WHAT YOU THINK EACH PARTY IS SAYING.

'I thought I heard you say that you wanted to be absolutely certain of taking your holiday in the summer? Is that right? And I think I heard you saying that it is essential that you take your holiday before 5th July.'

STEP 7　THEN DESCRIBE THE SCENARIO IN WHICH ALL THEIR NEEDS ARE MET.

'So what we are looking for is a holiday in the summer period before the 5th of July.'

STEP 8　THIS SHOULD MOVE THEM FORWARD ONE STEP. IF IT DOESN'T END THE DISAGREEMENT GO BACK TO THE FIRST STEP.

It's really all a matter of subsets. Draw a circle to represent all summer holidays

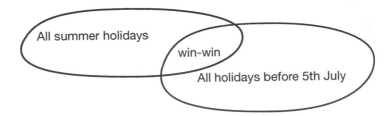

Fig. 2.13 Conflict resoution – seeking overlap for win-win solutions

and another to represent all holidays before the 5th of July.

Do they overlap? How would you describe the area of overlap? It looks as if it has to be the last week in June, the first week in July or nothing at all. This is the area of win-win.

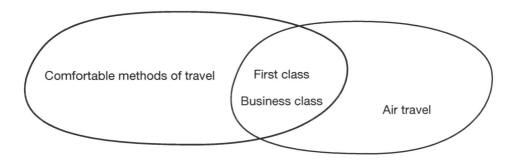

Fig. 2.14 Conflict resolution – identifying possible alternatives

Sometimes it is more complex. Just as you think you've got an area of overlap one of the stakeholders introduces another success criterion. 'How much is it going to cost?'

ESTABLISH THE BOUNDARIES OF THIS NEW CRITERION.

'What is the maximum you feel you could afford?'
'Three hundred pounds.'

GAIN AGREEMENT FROM BOTH THAT THIS IS A REASONABLE BOUN-
DARY. PLAY IT BACK TO THEM.

'Three hundred pounds, is this acceptable to both of you?'

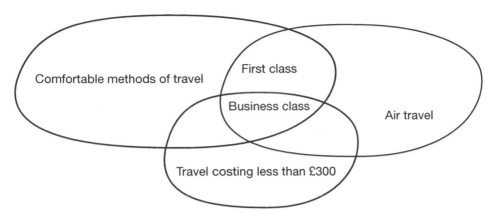

Fig. 2.15 Conflict resolution – narrowing down choices

Direct conflict

This is a lot harder to deal with. The paradox though, is that the reason that there is direct *conflict* is that you share the *same* objective.

You wish to have a successful trade, so on the one hand you must spend within your limits, which means that you must spend as little as you can get away with. On the other hand, the trader also wishes to have a successful trade which means that s/he must cover costs and must seek to charge as much as s/he can get away with. So s/he wants to charge as much as s/he can whilst you wish to pay as little as you can get away with.

You could negotiate if these two areas overlap. But since the situation is seen as direct conflict it will be hard to get the levels of openness required to figure out whether there is any chance of an overlap. There seems to be no overlap but that is often just in the way in which the problem is stated. Sometimes there is overlap in terms of the **reasons** why people are saying what they are.

In cases of direct conflict it is important to establish why the other party sees the world the way that they do. Developing a bubble diagram (Section 2.1.2 Blowing Bubbles) is an ideal way. Because of the lack of openness, you may have to work out why they want the outcome they want indirectly. If there is openness then start by asking why. Listen to the response and if there is overlap go back to the method for indirect conflict.

Direct conflict: Openness between parties.

STEP 1   ASK WHY THEY NEED THE OUTCOME AS THEY HAVE STATED.

159

'As little as you can get away with' could mean anything from nothing at all up to say ten Kenyan Shillings. 'As much as he can' could mean anything from his cost of eight Kenyan Shillings to 1000 (if selling to a gullible millionaire who has fallen in love with the piece). There is a chance of agreeing as long as our negotiations are in the right band. Any sum of money in that band represents a win-win.

Direct conflict: No openness between parties

STEP 1   MAKE YOUR OFFER AND LISTEN TO THE RESPONSE.

STEP 2   TRY TO DECIDE IF THERE IS A CHANCE OF OVERLAP.

STEP 3   IF YOU THINK THERE IS, REPEAT YOUR STARTING OFFER. MAKE THE STATEMENT AS BLAND AS POSSIBLE AND TALK HOLDING YOUR ARMS HALF OUTSTRETCHED WITH YOUR PALMS FACING UPWARD.

STEP 4   LISTEN TO THE RESPONSE. IF IT HAS CHANGED STICK TO YOUR LINE. CONTINUE WITH THIS UNTIL THE OTHER PARTY STARTS TO LOOK UNHAPPY THEN MOVE YOUR POSITION IN THEIR FAVOUR SLIGHTLY AND CLOSE THE DEAL.

STEP 5   IF THE RESPONSE HAS NOT CHANGED, MOVE YOUR POSITION SLIGHTLY.

STEP 6   ACCUSE THE OTHER PARTY OF BEING RIGID AND NOT GIVING ALTHOUGH YOU HAVE. REMAIN SILENT COUNT TO SIXTY AND THEN REPEAT THIS.

STEP 7   SAY HOW YOU, LIKE THE OTHER PARTY, WOULD LOVE TO HAVE A SUCCESSFUL OUTCOME. KEEP THIS UP UNTIL THEY MOVE THEIR POSITION.

STEP 8   WORK OUT HOW FAR THEY HAVE MOVED. THIS IS EASY WITH MONETARY TRANSACTIONS BUT HARDER WITH NON-MONETARY TRANSACTIONS. I FIND THAT MOST PEOPLE WILL GIVE AWAY ABOUT A FIFTH ON THE FIRST MOVE. SO NOW YOU KNOW WHAT THE FULL RANGE IS.

STEP 9   IT IS NOW IN YOUR POWER TO DEVELOP AN APPROPRIATE WIN-WIN SOLUTION.

Direct conflict: No openness and no overlap

Sometimes, there is **no** openness and **no** overlap. There is a gap between what one party wants and what another party wants. Often an enormous chasm. There is a solution though. How do you get across a chasm? You must bridge the gap. You do this by bartering.

STEP 1   OFFER THE OTHER PARTY SOMETHING WHICH YOU HAVE THE POWER
TO GIVE, WHICH IS OF LITTLE VALUE TO YOU, BUT IS OF LOTS OF
VALUE TO THEM.
IF POSSIBLE BRING IN A THIRD PARTY, SOMEONE WHO HAS A
DIFFERENT DEAL TO STRIKE WITH YOUR OPPONENT.

Your bubble diagram should give you clues on what you could offer.

In my giraffe example both I and the vendor tried this.

> The vendor looked round his stall. Walked to the back of the shop and returned
> with something. He showed it to me. It was a key ring with a small carved lion
> as the fob. It was not a brilliant carving. It looked more hacked than carved. He
> said that he would throw it in for free if I paid the full price for the giraffe
> carving.

> I explained that I was not an American (the popular misconception at the time
> was that Americans were made of money) and couldn't actually afford it but
> that I was on holiday with friends who also wanted to buy carvings. I said that I
> would bring my friends to his stall to have a look around. I added that they
> might not buy anything but at least they would visit him first – additional
> customers. He asked me when we would come round and I promised before the
> end of the week. We had a deal. He accepted my offer. As it happened my friend
> did not find anything they wanted at his stall but he was happy and so was I. A
> classic win-win.

Section 2.2.3
The Money

. . . Left to its own devices, each functional department will inevitably pursue approaches dictated by its professional orientation and the incentives of those in charge. However, the sum of these departmental approaches rarely equals the best strategy (for making money).
Michael E Porter

A very short time after you start the process of defining what your stakeholders think success is, you will suddenly realise that you understand the scope and needs of the project far better than anyone else. You will also recognise how parochial their visions are.

It is at this point, as project leader, *you* hold the **only** and **key** decision of the project.

'Should this project carry on or be stopped now?'

What you need to establish for yourself and on behalf of the organisation is whether the project appears to *legitimately* serve the goals of the organisation or whether it is an illegitimate exercise in *adventurism*. How do you answer this fairly for yourself? To answer this we must return to our understanding of the goals of the organisation. For the discussion I am only going to consider business organisations. I choose business organisations because it's easy to generalise about them, the reason being that they all have the same goal '. . . *to make money, both now and in the future'*. The choice of what the organisation's goals should be has already been made. It has been made by the *owners* of the business, the shareholders, who invested their **money** in the business, not to give it away, but in order to make **more money**.

For a project to legitimately serve the goal of the organisation it must help with this process of making money now and in the future. But how do organisations make money? Through sales? Through cost reduction? Through quality? What is the actual mechanism? A popular concept is that organisations make money through adding value.

This is an idea supported by standard accounting conventions (and even by the idea of value added tax). It works like this.

An organisation purchases services or raw materials (V); people in the organisation then work with the services, or machines work on the

162

materials. Step by step, each time you work on the service or raw material you add value (AV_1). So after four process steps the value of the work in progress (such as a part-built car or part-complete mortgage application) is $V + AV_1 + AV_2 + AV_3 + AV_4$. At the end of the process all the value has been added, $V+AV$, for which the sales price is S. Sometimes people add a margin (M) for profit and then say that $V + AV + M$ is the sales price. What does this mean? It means that a half-complete product is worth more (because it has a higher added value) than the raw materials (because no value has been added). This is reflected in the organisation's balance sheet. The stock or inventory is recorded as an asset and often conveys a message on the stage which the work in progress has reached.

It is **absolutely vital that you do not** use this standard convention for deciding whether a project will legitimately help the organisation with its goal. At an intuitive level you have probably guessed that this mechanism is wrong. It's a bit like suggesting for a project to build a bridge, that a half-complete bridge is more useful than no bridge at all . . . and that a half-completed bridge is half as useful as a complete bridge.

Most project costing conventions, such the use of net present value calculations, make this assumption implicitly.

But why is the mechanism wrong? Maybe we need to look at an example.

Imagine that it is your son's birthday and you have decided to buy him a lacquered fountain pen. You are standing in your local stationery shop describing what you are looking for. The shop assistant finally understands what you are after, reaches up to the shelf above and retrieves a box containing a pen of your description. You open the box but to your dismay you notice that the pen is irreparably damaged. It will not even write. It's obvious that it must have been damaged at about the mid point in its manufacture because it has been assembled, lacquered and boxed. It is of no use to you and doesn't even have any scrap value.

What happened to all the value that was added in the factory? It's obviously gone. Evaporated! But when did it evaporate? Was it (a) when you discovered that the pen was damaged? Was it (b) when the pen was actually damaged? Or was it (c) at some other time? Have you chosen? I'm sorry but all three are wrong! There was never any value there at all. The actual mechanism through which organisations make money is not by adding value. It is by adding cost and then keeping their fingers crossed that a customer will come along and take the product or service from them and give them back more money than they have actually spent.

Try this for a mechanism.

The organisation buys services or raw materials which costs it money (C). The organisation then works on these services or materials to convert them into a form in which they can sell them. To do this they must pay people and they must also pay for any machines or equipment, buildings, etc. that they need in order to carry out the conversion. (Sometimes they buy and own the equipment; sometimes they rent it, but it must still all be paid for.) All this additional cost is used for every stage in the conversion process. Money is spent and costs are added (-AC1).

By the end of the process the business has spent (-C-AC). We now hold our breath and keep our fingers crossed until someone buys it (S). Hopefully they leave us with a margin which represents our profits.

This **must** be the real mechanism, a mechanism in which it is the customer who decides whether or not we make money. If this was not the case we would simply make products/services – that is add value – and then put them in a warehouse! Why bother selling them?

Whenever **you** work on anything you **add costs**. The **customer decides** the **value** by giving you your money back. Hopefully, they give you back more than you spent.

So the business needs to be able to measure if it is making money. Most businesses do not measure whether they are making money now and in the future. It is traditional, instead to measure how much money was made in the previous year. How much money did we make (profit) and how does it compare to the amount we have had to leave in the business to make the money (return on investment)?

There is one small snag though. In the modern business world, change is occurring fast. So fast that our financial budgets (which look a year forward) are often adhered to closely for the first few months, after which their forecasts of spend and revenue begin to look ropy! How long is it from the time you put your budget to bed, to the time when you record the first variance? Some people claim that variances occur even before the budgets are finalised. That leaves me, and I suspect you, feeling distinctly uneasy about using a one year historic measure of profit and return on investment as a reasonable guide to whether or not the business is making money now and in the future.

To evaluate the legitimacy of projects in a modern business environment, we need to look for measures which look forwards and are dynamic. That is, we become more interested in the rates with which things occur than the sizes or amounts.

For you, as a project leader in this complex and rapidly changing business environment, many questions remain. How do you appraise a five year scheme when you are well aware that the goal posts will move during that period? What do you do if the project appears to be interlinked with others? How can you ensure that the money you spend will definitely lead to products or services that customers will part with their money for? How can you be sure that this money will make its way back to your business? How do you handle schemes that are merely defensive, one pound per month spent to avoid losing one pound per month sales? Do pay-back periods matter? Do they mean anything?

We need to think differently about what has the greatest and least impact on our ability to make money now and in the future.

Imagine coming across a shop in a back alley in your local town: a shop which sells money-making machines. Your initial reaction is one of stunned surprise, but at once you are approached by the shop assistant. What questions would you ask and in what sequence?

No. You do not ask how much the machines cost. That is not at all greedy.

No. You do not ask how much money they make. That is not quite greedy enough.

No. You do not ask to have the whole shop. That is far too greedy.

I would ask, in order of importance, *'Which one makes money fastest and for how long?'* (a £5 note in one minute is better than a £20 note in an hour, but don't forget to subtract the cost of paper and ink.) *'How fast do I need to spend to keep it running?'* (on labour, maintenance, etc.) *'How much does it cost to buy?'* (what investment must I make initially?) And finally, *'Is it legal?'*

The first three questions establish how much money I could make. The final one looks at the need to satisfy externally imposed conditions of business. The questions establish the real revenue rate, the operating expense rate and the investment tied up. Real revenue rate minus operating expense rate is a measure of how fast you are making money: a sort of profit per year figure. If you divide this figure by the amount of investment tied up you get a rate of return. Which gives you a complete sense of whether or not your choice of money making machine was a good one.

Imagine that you were a project leader in a major pharmaceutical company. Your research scientists have discovered a drug which is capable of producing a real revenue rate of £200 million each year. The project to build a facility to manufacture it is to cost £200,000 and will take a year to design and develop with your current in-house staff. What would you recommend to your company as it's best money making machine? A company with which I have worked now applies much of this approach to the development of new drugs. The company is happy to trade off project cost overruns for early completion in a ratio of about one million per month if the launch can be dragged forward. Quite simply, additional real revenue during the drug's early life cycle more than compensates for the work on the basis of project costs alone.

Being in the pharmaceutical industry, the company also has to satisfy the externally imposed conditions of the DHS/NHS or the US Food & Drugs Administration. It must understand fully when projects are set up simply to meet these externally imposed, necessary conditions. For this client, drug launches are usually linked to national launches by sales forces across the globe. These national sales teams are often involved in a number of other simultaneous promotions and initiatives, and since all markets vary, it is the timeliness of the project, not the absolute time, that is the measure of success.

Now let us return to your problem of deciding how legitimate your project is. Clearly this is an important question which can only be answered by you. To be legitimate a project must directly do **at least one** of the following:

Maintain or increase the rate at which the business makes money now and in the future.

Maintain or reduce the rate at which the business needs to spend money now and in the future.

Maintain or reduce the amount of money tied up in the business now and in the future.

Support or provide a solution to a necessary or externally imposed condition.

Does your project do any of these directly? If it does not, you will need to extend its scope and make it a *complete* and *legitimate* project.

For example, a project which provides hand-held computerised customer database equipment for the sales force sounds exciting. Sales people will be better able to track customer needs. They will be more efficient and have more time available. They will be able to avoid re-entering data and introducing misspelt names, etc.

However, this project is still not legitimate unless more sales are made using the extra time. Or the number (and cost) of the sales force is reduced. Or the sales force has more time to provide a better level of service that either the customer so values the service that it prevents him switching supplier, or it enables us to charge more for the service. Or fewer goods are lost by being sent to the wrong address. If none of these developments are within the scope of the deliverables of the project, the project is not complete and will not give a legitimate outcome.

To make the project complete you will need to extend its scope to cover at least one of these favourable outcomes. If it is not possible to extend the scope or if it does not meet with at least one of the four criteria, kill it now! Save yourself the headache. Save yourself the cost, remember doing anything in business costs you money or time, and by not doing anything, *improve* the performance of your business.

The process of making a project complete and legitimate by altering or extending its scope usually highlights additional stakeholders which should be added to your stakeholder maps (Section 2.2.1.).

IMPLICATIONS FOR PROJECTS

Rules of thumb

1. Plan your project so that you spend money as late as possible but get revenue as early as possible.

2. If your project is addressing a necessary or imposed condition always do it at minimum cost.

3. Closely manage projects where there is more than a year of spending before revenues come in. Always organise such projects in phases with opt outs. It's best if, at each opt out, you can retain or gain business benefits.

4. Be very careful with open projects aimed at reducing running costs or investment levels.

5. Legitimate projects usually rely on end users changing their ways of working. It is important to explain legitimacy to end users.

6. If you have a choice of projects rank them in terms of which of the 'money making machine' questions they answer.

7. It makes better business sense to kill a project at the start, than in the middle.

Section 2.2.4
Balancing Stakeholder Expectations

Success is relative:
It is what we can make of the mess we have made of things.
T. S. Elliot

EXPECTATIONS AND REALITY ARE BOTH VARIABLE

How do other people decide whether or not something we have done meets their success criteria? The logical and judgmental ones among us will reply that it depends on whether or not we meet the written and measurable success criteria. But is that right?

> I fly a lot. I get very impatient about flights which take off late. I've noticed that with some airlines, the moment that they think that they are going to be late taking off they announce the delay. They then regularly keep you up to date on progress. And although the flight leaves an hour late you have been able to pace yourself, maybe spending time in the bookshop or restaurant. Other airlines deafen you with silence. Not only do they not warn you of the possibility of lateness they just keep you hanging around for the full hour and then apologise once you are aboard the plane.

The measured facts are that both airlines have kept me waiting for the same length of time. And yet I tend to feel far more dissatisfied with the second airline than with the first. Why has this happened? What is the difference? The difference is that the first airline reset what I was expecting to happen and did so at the earliest opportunity. Reality had changed and they lowered my expectations to match reality. I was less happy with the second service because my expectation was that I would get on the plane at a certain time and that did not happen. Reality happened and made sure that my expectations were not met.

> Imagine it's mid winter and you get home early one evening. The rest of the family, like you, are getting a bit fed up with spending all these long dark evenings at home. It would be a great break if you could get out. Someone suggests going to the pictures. You haven't been to the pictures for years but it seems a good idea. You look in the local newspaper at the listings. None of the titles on show mean anything to anyone but you still decide to go. You arrive and look at the posters outside the cinema. There's one with a man in a hat called *Indy John and the Mystical Cat*. You go in and watch it.

Did you enjoy it? Chances are that you did. It was OK.

Now imagine that for the last month you have kept hearing about a new film called *Indy John and the Mystical Cat*. Jokes are made about it in meetings. You hear people discussing it around the coffee machine. There was even a cartoon circulated which depicted the Chief Exec. as a cat with a caption saying 'I've got the Indy up me'. The last straw comes when your boss walks past your desk whistling (music from the film), stops, turns round and asks you whether you have seen *Indy John and the Mystical Cat*? His parting words are 'You really must see *Indy John and the Mystical Cat*, it's brilliant!' Now you haven't been to the pictures for years, but you decide you must. So you get home and announce to the family that you will be taking them to see *Indy John and the Mystical Cat*. You phone to book and discover that the earliest that you can get seats is a month away so you wait for the appointed time and go to see the film. It lasts 90 minutes.

Did you enjoy it? Chances are that you did not. In fact you could have sworn that it lasted three hours! What happened? Did the projectionist spot you in the queue and swap the reels of the original film for reels of the ultra-boring export version? No! I don't think so. Quite simply, reality stayed the same but this time your expectations had been moved.

Balancing stakeholder expectations is about realising that reality rarely matches expectations. It may surpass or disappoint. **Both are wrong**. Think of it as a simple balance with a handful of uneven sized stones on both sides. You can if you wish place additional stones on either side. The object is to keep both sides level at all times. Unfortunately, an invisible hand (belonging to a chap called Fate) keeps adding to or removing stones from the side of reality.

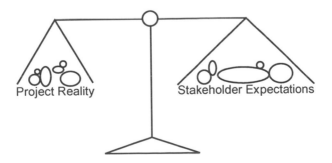

Fig. 2.16 Balancing reality and expectations – keeping both sides level

Sounds simple. So how is it that common project expressions include; 'What I was expecting was . . .', 'I don't remember agreeing to that!', 'What I agreed to was . . .', 'Where on earth did that come from?' and 'I guess that's what you are used to but it isn't good enough in this case'?

EXPECTATIONS CHANGE WITH TIME

The odds are stacked against you in projects and unless you realise this, you cannot balance expectations. Let me use a non-project related example you have experienced dozens of times but perhaps never analysed, to explain.

It's mid afternoon and looks as if your business meeting will go on until the early evening. You are trying to work out a deal with some visitors from out of town. You suggest going out for a meal at the end of the day. Your suggestion is greeted enthusiastically. There is a brief discussion about the type of food you should go for. You decide on Italian. You don't know any good Italian restaurants so you ask your secretary to ask around the office for recommendations of an Italian restaurant within walking distance, and carry on your discussions. Your secretary comes back with two suggestions. They both sound fine. You ask your secretary to find out if either one can accommodate six for dinner. Five minutes later your secretary comes in to tell you that both restaurants have been called. 'Both?' you question. 'Yes, both.' comes back the reply. The first one took ages to answer the phone and when it was answered the reply was a gruff 'What do you want? Six people? OK. But they would have to be on time or else their table would be given away!' The second answered straight away, were polite and were, '. . . happy to accommodate the party of six' and it would be, '. . . no problem if they were a little late in concluding their business.'

Which one do you choose? Why?

You set off to walk to the restaurant. It is in the up-market part of town.

What thoughts are going through your mind? (To do with cost?)

You arrive and are kept waiting at the door for four minutes before any one comes up to invite you to be seated.

What are you thinking about the service of the establishment?

You are seated, offered drinks and the menu. After a little deliberation, you choose. Then you have to wait. Just after the first course is served the Maitre'D comes up to your table and asks 'Is everything to your satisfaction?' You reply as we always do, especially if asked early in the meal, 'Yes, fine."

This technique of asking for feedback before any milestones are complete is a trick used by cheap restaurants; it saves them coming round later when you might be prepared to give them a harder time.

> You come to the end of the meal. It's been good, not great. You ask for the bill. Ten minutes later you ask again. The bill finally arrives. It looks like a lot of money.

In general, the better the meal the longer the restaurant can afford to keep you waiting for the bill. If the service and food were mediocre anything other than prompt presentation of the bill is likely to make you feel, when it finally arrives, that you have been completely ripped off.

> You get up to leave. As you walk out the Maitre'D asks you if you have had a pleasant evening and invites you to visit them again. You are handed a box of matches to make sure that you can remember where you had the meal and can go back to them at a later date if you wish.

Now look at it from the restaurateur's point of view.

> The phone rings. You are woken up with a start. This puts you in a foul mood. You are worn out. After all you were up late last night. You snarl into the phone, 'What do you want?' Six people! What happens if they don't turn up. It would tie up two good tables for a whole evening. That's what happened last night. You decide to be firm. 'You will have to be on time or else your table will be given away!'

Or . . .

> The 'phone by the bed rings. You answer it quickly. You have been up the night before, but recognise that to the person calling that's *your* problem. You want the business and try to sound bright and helpful. Six people! Useful if they start to use your restaurant on an ongoing basis for post-meeting dinners. Of course, like most people they wish to arrive at 8.30 when you are most busy, because everyone is arriving then. You agree, hoping that they will be late.
>
> The evening starts slowly and then gets busier and busier. It's a warm evening and lots of people have decided to eat out. Out of the corner of your eye you spot a group of people waiting to be seated but you are busy with other customers. Eventually you show them to their seats and hand them menus. A few minutes later you take their orders. You take them to the chef in the kitchen. The chef is overworked, the orders are piling up. You try to help but you can't really. You don't have the skills. You take them the starter. As usual everyone has forgotten what they ordered. A few minutes later you ask them if everything is

171

OK. They say, 'Yes' and you assume that they mean it. You rush off back to the kitchen to see what you can do to speed things up.

You have been rushed off your feet all evening. The group of six ask for the bill. You are more concerned with finishing things off than with sorting out the bill. After all, they've had the meal now and can't leave until they have paid. As they leave you try to sell on. You give them a box of matches with the address and ask them to call back again.

The project is rather closed in this case. The different stages are separate and discrete.

STAGE FOR DRIVER	STATE OF DRIVER	STAGE FOR DELIVERER	STATE OF DELIVERER
(Client, Sponsor End User, etc.)	(Client, Sponsor End User, etc.)	(Project team, Subcontractor, Supplier) Supplier)	(Project team, Subcontractor,
Selection.	Busy collecting information. Setting initial expectations.	None.	Idle. Unaware of what is round the corner.
Access. First point of contact.	Expectations gain substance. If not met may return to selection.	**Definition** starts. **Awareness** of start of project.	Busy. Preparation starts.
Response time.	Idle but impatient.	**Definition** continues. **Planning** may start.	Busy getting ready to deliver.
Impact.	Real contact established.		
Delivery definition.	Judgmental. Selection of deliverables. Expectations getting set in stone.	**Definition** complete.	Very, very, busy.
None.	Idle. Waiting impatiently or may forget all about what they are expecting.	**Planning** and **resourcing.**	Very, very, busy in project team. Little time for other stakeholders
Delivery. You are receiving the outputs of the project. Sometimes you receive nothing until right at the end.	Anticipatory. Busy when the project delivers, e.g. at milestones, otherwise idle. Expectations are met or mismatched at each milestone. Excellent opportunity to blow the whole project.	**Implementation.**	Very, very, busy. All focus is on getting the jobs done. Milestone meetings seen as a necessary evil where outcome stakeholders fuss.
Delivery close out.	Anxiety about costs. Anxiety about hand-over. Any expectations mismatch is seen as a disaster to be dealt with immediately.	**Hand over** and **close out.**	Very, very, busy tying up loose ends of the task. Little time for non-team stakeholders.

So whenever you are at your most busy at getting the job done is **exactly** the *same time* as you are needed to re-balance stakeholders' expectations.

THE STARTING ODDS ARE STACKED AGAINST YOU

How do stakeholders form their expectations in the first place? How did you form your expectations of the restaurant meal in the first place? From previous trips to other restaurants. From what other people who had visited the restaurant said about it. From your companions' view on what Italian restaurants are like. Their views might be very different if they were Italian themselves. And finally from the few interactions you had with the restaurant owner and staff. These were the only chances that the restaurant owner had to influence your expectations directly.

What your stakeholders expect of projects is formed in the same way. From previous projects they have witnessed or been involved in. Stories they have heard of great project successes or failures and the consequences. From each other. The team have an expectation which depends on the client.

For example, in one industry I worked in, team members saw pharmaceutical clients as rich and disorganised and treated them with disdain. Whilst they viewed medium sized manufacturing companies as miserly and penny pinching and so spent all their time trying to find ways to extract more money from them even though they usually started with a fair deal.

The sponsor has expectations set by knowing who is in the team and so on. Finally, the interactions they have with you provide the **only** opportunity you have to influence their expectations. *One* out of *many* others. This is partly why your ability to communicate effectively has such an influence over project success.

As project leader you have two simultaneous tasks. *You have to shape reality – the* project deliverables – to meet the hard and soft success criteria, and *you also have to reshape expectations* on an ongoing basis to ensure that they meet with reality. But there are far many more influences on your stakeholders' expectations than just you and what you tell them. They have preconceptions and they have their expectations remodelled by each other and by actual reality. There are many channels, of which yours is only one. You therefore need as much leverage as possible. Section 2.3.4. Communications Strategies, focuses on some of the strategies you can adopt in order to keep your stakeholders in balance through communications.

MAINTAINING BALANCE

STEP 1   GO BACK TO YOUR STAKEHOLDER MAP (SECTION 2.2.1 MAPPING STAKEHOLDERS) MARK IT UP.

STEP 2   MAKE THREE GROUPS OF STAKEHOLDERS (REMEMBER THE SAND CASTLE IN CHAPTER SEVEN)

- UNDERLINE IN RED: THOSE WHO MUST BE INFORMED OF ANY CHANGES IN ADVANCE OF THE CHANGE (USUALLY THE DRIVERS OR OUTCOME STAKEHOLDERS, CLIENT END USER OR SPONSOR).

- MARK WITH A RED SPOT: THOSE WHO CAN BE INFORMED OF CHANGES AT THE TIME OF THE CHANGE WITHOUT GENERATING SIGNIFICANT WAVES. (USUALLY THE DIRECT DELIVERERS, THE TEAM AND OTHER DIRECT CONTRIBUTORS).

- NO ADDITIONAL MARKS: THOSE WHO YOU CAN GET AWAY WITH INFORMING OF CHANGES AFTER THE EVENT.

STEP 3   SCHEDULE IN ADVANCE (NOW) REGULAR MEETINGS WITH THE FIRST GROUP.

STEP 4   MAKE UP A 'COPY TO' LIST FOR ALL THE STAKEHOLDERS IN THE SECOND CATEGORY.

Section 2.3
PLANNING AND CO-ORDINATING

Perspective use it or lose it.
Richard Bach

I once attended an International Project Management Conference in Vienna. As part of the conference there was an exhibition for suppliers. There were professional project management consultants, book stands, but by far the largest area was taken up by computer companies offering software packages. These days, project planning has been reduced to a computer package. For about sixty dollars you can buy project planning software. I remember reading the blurb for one such package. It claimed to solve all your project planning and reporting needs. Amazing! And all for sixty dollars. I walked through the exhibition and then went off to listen to a paper on project success and failure. The statistics were not good. Depending on how you cut it, between 30% and 80% of projects had major problems. I felt like telling the speaker not to worry because from now on, for only sixty dollars, the problem of project planning and control would be banished and never ever seen again. I didn't though.

'Anyone who does not realise that *the true nature of planning is to* **continuously gain and maintain perspective** and that the *true nature of co-ordination and control is to* **spread and use the perspective amongst stakeholders**, and that the two things are two **separate** processes, will find it difficult to consistently succeed with projects.'

Section 2.3.1
Sticky Steps™: A Step by Step Approach to Planning Change

Even a thousand mile journey begins with a single step.
Be sure that the step is in the right direction.
Zen Buddhist saying

What is the true nature of planning? By now, you will agree that planning has nothing to do with time schedules or bar charts. Those simply represent the ways in which we communicate the plan to our stakeholders. Planning can be little more than the process of gaining and maintaining perspective. If *accomplished change is change chosen carefully* then we need methods to help us to choose our change carefully. I want you to think of avoiding having to do everything, and to concentrate on the few barriers which, if you choose and get over them, will mean that you have accomplished your change. But how can we find these barriers? I can see how you can spot barriers if the chunk is closed. They are in the same place as last time. But what if you are walking in a fog?

The only way I know of to plan for all types of project, walking in the fog, going on a quest, making a movie or indeed painting-by-numbers, is to use perspective. Imagine that you were at the end of a long journey in which your project had been completed. Look back at it and describe what you did. The **Sticky Steps** approach works in this way. It allows you to look backwards, going from a complete and Herculean task which is almost too large to contemplate, to tiny little steps which you could wake up on Monday and do. I invented this method because I could not find any other way of planning lost in the fog-type projects. The name comes from the fact that you use post-it notes as the main kit.

The example I shall use is of a 'fog' project. But it will work on all types.

> I was once approached by a delegate on one of my courses. He came up to me looking particularly anxious. 'My boss,' he said 'has told me that I am to install something he calls 'business process re-engineering' in our business. He sees this as my major goal and wants me to drop everything and get on with it.'
>
> 'I see.' I replied. 'Well, what's the problem?'
>
> 'I haven't got the faintest idea what he wants. I tried to ask him but I soon realised that he doesn't have much of a clue either and I've never run a project before. What do I do? Where do I start?'

177

It sounded to me like he was in a bit of a fog.

'What did you say that he had asked you to do?' I questioned.

'Install business process re-engineering.' he said flatly.

'What would you *have had to have done in order to have* "Installed business process re-engineering"?' I asked.

'Found out what on earth it is!' came back the bemused answer.

'Anything else?' I pressed.

'No.' He replied. 'No, that will do just for starters.'

I kept probing. 'And what would you *have had to have done in order to have* "Found out what on earth it is"?'

'I guess,' he said, 'that I could look in the library.'

'Anything else?' I asked.

'I could find out if there are any tutors who know about it.'

'Anything else?'

'I could ask you.'

I smiled and replied. 'I know, but I'll only talk to you after you have done some homework of your own.'

We seemed to have gone from something nebulous, a chunk of change too large to comprehend, to something which he could go away and do.

The next day he came back. 'I've made some progress but I'm stuck again.' 'What are you stuck on?' 'I now know what the words mean but I still need to work out exactly what to do. 'Do you still have the same objective?' I asked.

'Yesish.'

'Yesish?'

'Well,' he replied thoughtfully, 'I now think that the objective is actually not to do with jargon at all. It is really to develop new ways in which to work together across the organisation.'

'So in order to have "developed new ways in which to work together across the organisation" you would have had to have . . .?' I let it hang in the air. 'What would you *have had to have done?*'

There was a short pause, after which he replied, 'Found out which processes we currently have, and established if they are good or bad.'

'Anything else?'

'Brought my boss up to speed.'

'So, what else would you *have had to have done in order to have* "found out which processes we currently run and established if they are good or bad".'

'Brought my colleagues up to speed.'

'Anything else?'

'Not for now,' he replied.

'So what would you *have had to have done to have* "found out what processes you currently have and established if they are good or bad"?'

'Attended a seminar.'

I frowned. 'That doesn't quite fit with the sentence, does it? Just say it to yourself out loud.'

'OK. If you insist. In order to have "found out what processes I currently have and established if they are good or bad I would have had to have attended a seminar". You're right, it doesn't fit.'

'It might have fitted with the earlier sentence, when you were trying to install something you didn't understand, but it doesn't here. Lets start again.' I suggest. 'In order to have "found out which processes we currently run and established if they are good or bad" *we would have had to have*?'

'Followed through the business to establish the chains of activities we routinely carry out.'

'Anything else?'

'Recorded them.' he said.

'Anything else?'

'Discussed them with the people involved in them.'

I took his hand, shook it warmly and said, 'Good luck!'

STICKY STEPS™

Part One: Working out the steps

STEP 1 TRY TO WORK OUT THE 'WHAT' OF YOUR CHUNK. IF YOU ARE LEADING AN OPEN PROJECT JUST GUESS THE 'WHAT'. YOU CAN CHANGE IT LATER.

STEP 2 WRITE ON A LARGE SHEET, FLIP CHART OR WALL WHITE BOARD, '*IN ORDER TO HAVE . . .*'

STEP 3 WRITE DOWN THE WHAT OF YOUR CHUNK ON A POST-IT NOTE. START WITH A **VERB** IN THE **PAST** TENSE. FOR EXAMPLE, '*INSTALLED BUSINESS PROCESS RE-ENGINEERING*'.

STEP 4 CONTINUE WITH THE SENTENCE YOU HAVE WRITTEN DOWN ON THE LARGE SHEET. WRITE '*WE WOULD HAVE HAD TO HAVE . . .*'.

STEP 5 IMAGINE THAT YOU HAVE ACTUALLY COMPLETED THE CHUNK AND YOU ARE LOOKING BACKWARDS IN TIME. WRITE ON A POST-IT NOTE ANYTHING YOU CAN IMAGINE YOU WOULD HAVE HAD TO HAVE DONE.

STEP 6 PLACE THE POST-IT ON THE BOARD UNDERNEATH THE SENTENCE TO THE RIGHT HAND SIDE.

STEP 7 ASK YOURSELF IF THERE IS ANYTHING ELSE?

STEP 8 IF THERE IS, WRITE IT DOWN ON ANOTHER POST-IT NOTE.

STEP 9 GO BACK TO STEP 7 UNTIL THERE IS NOTHING FURTHER TO ADD.

STEP 10 CHOOSE ONE OF THE STICKIES AND USE IT TO REPLACE THE ORIGINAL 'WHAT' AT THE END OF 'IN ORDER TO HAVE . . .' PLACE THE ORIGINAL 'WHAT' IN THE TOP RIGHT HAND CORNER OF THE BOARD.

STEP 11 NOW MOVE ALL THE OTHER YELLOW STICKIES TO THE LEFT HAND SIDE OF THE BOARD.

STEP 12 GO BACK TO STEP 5.

STEP 13 REPEAT THIS LOOP UNTIL THE STICKIES HAVE TASKS WRITTEN ON THEM. TASKS. THAT IS, THINGS WHICH YOU COULD WAKE UP ON MONDAY MORNING AND DECIDE YOU WERE GOING TO DO AND JUST DO.

STEP 14 MOVE THE TASKS TO THE TOP RIGHT HAND CORNER OF THE BOARD.

STEP 15 DISCARD ALL THE STICKIES YOU GENERATED IN THE LOOP GETTING TO THE TASKS.

STEP 16   TAKE THE NEXT STICKER FROM THE BOTTOM LEFT HAND SIDE.

STEP 17   GO BACK TO STEP 5.

STEP 18   WHEN YOU HAVE WORKED YOUR WAY THROUGH ALL THE LOOPS
THE FIRST PART OF THE PROCESS IS OVER.

I have made three sketches to illustrate what the board should look like at the start after Step 4:

In order to have ...

| developed new ways in which to work together across the organisation |

Fig. 2.17 Sticky steps 1 – guess the 'what' of the project

And after Step 7:

In order to have ...

developed new ways in which to work together across the organisation

We would have had to have ....

| Found out which processes we currently run and established if they are good or bad. | Brought my boss up to speed. | Brought my colleagues up to speed. | Followed through the business to establish the chains of activities we routinely carry out |

Fig. 2.18 Sticky steps 2 – guess the large steps (subprojects)

And after step 10:

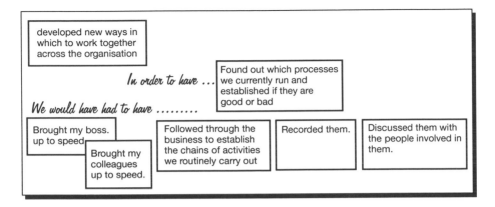

Fig. 2.19 Sticky steps 1 – guess the small steps (tasks)

Section 2.3.2
Pacing Yourself

*Anticipation is not clever; they're always running late. The problem is
you never know how long you will wait.*
Ernest Obeng

By now you will have a pile of tasks to be undertaken. If you are to work
with others you will need to invite them to walk through the sticky steps
themselves.

With open projects, you will need to walk through the steps above on your
own first and then go through it with other stakeholders. Why? No: it's not
so that you can control the process. It's far more fundamental. In a truly
open project you will not know who to invite to the planning session. If you
first run through your sticky steps on your own you will recognise from the
tasks you generate many of the most appropriate stakeholders. You will
then need to invite them to participate in the process.

A pile of tasks on it's own is totally useless. How often have you found
yourself part of someone else's plan? You know the feeling. When they
hand you the bar chart, neatly printed out with your name on it, or the
action list. It's not in your handwriting, it's incomprehensible and even
worse, it's not part of your personal organising system.

We all have systems ranging from 'to do' lists to diaries to sophisticated
electronic personal organisers. Any action which does not become an
integral part of our own personal system tends to get forgotten. As project
leader it is your job to **continuously gain and maintain perspective** and
spread and use the perspective amongst stakeholders. Your
stakeholders must see your chunk of change in the perspective of their own
lives. Anything that you can do to transfer the project perspective to a
corporate perspective is good. For example it is more important that they
write the tasks in their diary than that you have the tasks written up in a
neat bar chart.

You will also address another problem with modern business projects. The
problem is that it is increasingly unlikely that you will have a 100 per cent
dedicated team. In most modern projects, people are only giving you part of
their time. Increasingly this is becoming true, even of commercial projects,
as companies make more use of contract and specialist staff. These staff are
brought in to deliver a specific project activity or provide a skill. The
company's own core staff span the projects, each acting as an octopus with
many fingers in many pies. And as we begin to look at projects which are

not of the painting-by-numbers variety we find that we can not reasonably estimate the time for each task. And worse still, the time most tasks take is very variable.

This high level of sharing of a limited amount of resources also helps explain why critical path methods will not be covered in this section. Critical path methods start off assuming that you have an infinite amount of resource, all the resources you need in fact. It then establishes the best order for tasks to be done. In most modern business projects it is more important to schedule the resources than to schedule the tasks. Resource constraints are more common than dependency constraints.

Anyone who is wedded to the use of critical path analysis should try the quiz below.

William and Victor have to carry out a project. William can do jobs which Victor can't but Victor is undaunted by this because he can do things which William can't. Left to get on and fully dedicate their time to one job they have suggested the minimum time they would have to spend on each task. If they have to stop and start then it will take them about twice as long to complete the job. Victor is responsible for three jobs which can be done right at the start. William's work depends on Victor's work being complete. I have summarised this below

Task:	Duration:	Physically depends on:	Physically leads to:	Done by:
A1	60	START	A2	VICTOR
B1	25	START	B2	VICTOR
C1	5	START	C2	VICTOR
A2	5	A1	END	WILLIAM
B2	30	B1	END	WILLIAM
C2	45	C1	END	WILLIAM

a. What is the critical path?
b. What is the fastest time to completion based on the critical path?
c. What is the realistic shortest actual time it will take to get the project complete?
d. What is the best sequence of jobs? Is it the one suggested by the answer to a.?

Answers
a. There isn't one in the strictest sense. You probably worked out A1-A2
b. 65 days. As usual you schedule tasks first assuming infinite resource and

then correct for resources at above 100% by smoothing.

c. 95 days. (You probably started with the critical path A1-A2 which gave you a result of 160 [for Victor; A1-B1-C1] or 140 [for Victor; A1-C1- B1].)

d.

Victor	−C1	−B1	−A1	finished	
William	WAIT	−C2	−B2	−WAIT	−A2

PS. This would also be the best way to get momentum up on the project. In real life you would want them working alongside each other as soon as possible.

(See References: *The Race*, Goldratt E, and Fox R.)

In most business situations you do not have infinite resources. You may, if the project economics allow, go out and get some more. But what actually holds you up is your access to resources, people, special skills, kit etc. In 1987 I published a paper which described a technique I called PACE analysis. The technique looked at the use of time for economic gain. Since then I have approached scheduling on the basis of: **resource first-task second**. I assume that as a project leader you can either chase the tasks or manage the people who then manage the tasks for you. The project is like a relay race, but with many runners running both in series and in parallel. Stakeholders pass on the baton from one person to another. A sort of game. A sort of adult tag where the objective is to pass the baton on to the next person as soon as you can. For the process to run effectively every task should have a primary owner. This must be the case, even if the task is actually to be carried out by the whole team together.

The other reason for considering resources first is that modern chunks of change can be very variable. This means that addressing the tasks first tends to overload your resources. Overloading generally means that people are working flat out and yet nothing comes out.

Have you ever had the experience whilst driving along a crowded motorway, when all of a sudden, out of the blue, you have to slam your brakes on as hard as possible. You then crawl along for a short distance and then the traffic speeds up. There is no sign of what has caused your delay. No accident. No roadworks. What caused the need to decelerate so violently? How does this happen? It's actually the combination of the first two Laws of Change. The cars are so close that the speed of one car influences the one behind. They are dependent on each other. This is true for the whole long chain of cars up to yours. One change is very likely to lead to another. Then a car near the front speeds up. *Adds a change* slowly. One after another, the whole chain of cars speeds up. Only at about the time when roughly half the cars have sped up to match the new speed, a car near the front slows down. Not a lot, only slightly. It takes a while for the car behind this one to notice the slowing down, so the second car has slightly less time to brake. So the second car slows down slightly faster. The third car in the chain experiences a bigger change in the need to slow down and has even less time to react, and so it carries on. By the time it gets to you, you have to go from 70 miles an hour to a dead stop in a second! The first two laws conspire to send shock waves down the chain of cars. The same is true in projects. Modern projects, like all projects do have chains of dependent events. Modern projects are also task-time variable. This means that if you succeed in scheduling more tasks than the resources can cope with, you simply send a series of shock waves through the organisation. Much activity occurs in the organisation, in-trays back up, but little comes out.

In practical terms, the way round this is to insert time buffers into your scheduling process. A bit like leaving a large gap between you and the car in front, a *time buffer* should be inserted, almost as a task in its own right, just before any really key or scarce resource needs to be called into your project. This will make the best use of the resource for the whole organisation. A time buffer must also be inserted anywhere that two or more tasks need to be completed before further work can be carried out. I am also very wary of any resource which, on paper seems to be loaded to more than about 70 per cent. A paper estimate of seventy per cent is usually optimistic and is equivalent to a realistic loading of 100 per cent. This means the cars are too close.

STICKY STEPS™

Part Two: Gaining Buy-in, Communicating the plan and Scheduling tasks

STEP 1 INVITE THE KEY STAKEHOLDERS TO PART ONE OF STICKY STEPS. REMIND THEM TO BRING THEIR DIARIES.

STEP 2 CARRY OUT PART ONE OF THE STICKY STEPS WITH THE KEY STAKEHOLDERS.

STEP 3 ON A SECOND BOARD WRITE ALL THE NAMES OF YOUR KEY STAKEHOLDERS VERTICALLY DOWN THE LEFT HAND SIDE.

STEP 4 WRITE A TIME AXIS ALONG THE TOP HORIZONTALLY. CHOOSE THE APPROPRIATE TIME FRAME FOR THE TYPE OF CHANGE:
CLOSED – ACTUAL DATES/TIMES UP TO THE FINAL DATE OR DROP DEAD DATE.
OPEN – THREE COLUMNS LABELLED; THIS WEEK (OR MONTH), NEXT WEEK (OR MONTH) AND SOON. CHOOSE THE TIME SCALE TO REPRESENT HOW FAR YOU CAN SEE IN THE FOG. IF YOU CAN SEE THE NEXT MONTH WITH CERTAINTY USE THE ONE WEEK SCALE. IF YOU CAN SEE THE NEXT SIX MONTHS THEN USE THE MONTH SCALE.

STEP 5 NUMBER ALL THE STICKIES WITH TASKS ON THEM (ANY NUMBERING SYSTEM WILL DO AS LONG AS IT IS SIMPLE).

STEP 6 LIFT A STICKY OFF THE FIRST BOARD AND READ IT OUT TO THE GROUP.

STEP 7 ASK 'WHO SHOULD DO THIS?' WAIT FOR A VOLUNTEER OR FOR SOMEONE TO BE VOLUNTEERED.

STEP 8 ASK 'WHEN SHOULD IT BE DONE? WHEN SHOULD IT START?' IF THERE ARE ANSWERS WRITE THEM ON THE TOP RIGHT HAND SIDE OF THE POST-IT.

STEP 9 ASK 'WHO PASSES YOU THE BATON? IF YOU KNOW AND IT IS OBVIOUS, WRITE ON THE LEFT HAND CORNER WHO PASSES THE BATON (AND THE NUMBER OF THE STICKY, IF KNOWN).

STEP 10 ASK 'WHO DO YOU PASS THE BATON TO?' IF YOU KNOW AND IT IS OBVIOUS WRITE ON THE RIGHT HAND CORNER THE PERSON THE BATON IS PASSED TO (AND THE NUMBER OF THE STICKY IF KNOWN)

STEP 11 TRANSFER A STICKY FROM THE FIRST BOARD TO THE SECOND BOARD. PLACE IT AGAINST THE NAME AND TIME.

STEP 12   ASK THE PERSON INVOLVED IN THE STICKY, 'HAVE YOU GOT THAT?'
ENCOURAGE THEM TO PUT IT IN THEIR DIARY.

STEP 13   GO BACK TO STEP 6 AND REPEAT UNTIL ALL THE STICKIES HAVE
BEEN TRANSFERRED.

STEP 14   LOOK AT THE BOARD. ASK PEOPLE WHAT THEY THINK THEIR WORK
LOAD IS. IF THEY SAY THAT IT IS MORE THAN 70 PER CENT INSERT A
TIME BUFFER. USE YOUR JUDGEMENT TO WORK OUT HOW LONG
THE TIME BUFFER SHOULD BE.

STEP 15   LOOK AT THE BOARD. WHEREVER MORE THAN ONE ACTIVITY MUST
BE COMPLETE BEFORE THE NEXT ACTIVITIES CAN BE STARTED,
INSERT A TIME BUFFER. USE YOUR JUDGEMENT TO WORK OUT HOW
LONG THE TIME BUFFER SHOULD BE.

STEP 16   (FOR NEATNESS MANIACS ONLY) GET THE SCHEDULE DRAWN UP
NEATLY.

Section 2.3.3
The Risk of Being So Near . . . Yet So Far:
Co-ordination, Control and Risk

*In America any boy may become president and I guess it's just one of the
risks he takes.*
Adlai Stevenson

How come the thing that always messes up the whole project is a small,
unforeseen problem that you hadn't really considered that much? It's
almost like a small child clamouring for attention.

> I once came across a multi-million pound aerospace project which was running
> late. The project leader and sponsor were very concerned. They were worried
> that they had a large number of very expensive engineers who were sitting on
> their hands with nothing to do. That sounds bad but it was actually worse.
> Engineers are bright people, so my bet is, what was actually happening was
> that they were inventing a bunch of really difficult problems to solve later. The
> cost of being held up was several hundred thousand pounds a day. What was
> the cause of the delay? What was so crucial and yet so hard to resolve? It turned
> out to be a subcontract of a subcontractor who was manufacturing a new
> electronic component. It was a component that they had never manufactured
> before. But since no one else knew how to manufacture the part and they put in
> the lowest priced tender they won the bid. There was one small problem
> though. They had underbid and in the process of producing the component had
> run out of cash and gone bankrupt. It was a minor component and not on the
> critical path (see Section 2.3.2. Pacing Yourself, for critique of critical path
> analysis). No one had paid it much attention. The project came in nine months
> late and two and a half million pounds overspent with a disgruntled team.

What is the real problem here? Is it planning, co-ordination, control or risk
management? I think all four. We know what Planning is (see Section
2.3.1. Sticky Steps). But how do you control someone over whom you do not
have direct authority? How do you co-ordinate if there are a multitude of
tasks and you don't know which could really sting you? And how do you
manage risks? What is a risk anyway? Doesn't everything have a level of
risk?

What is the problem we are really trying to solve? We are trying to **spread
and use the perspective amongst stakeholders**. We want to be able to
understand what can really damage the success of the project. In a rapidly
changing chaotic world, assessing risk becomes meaningless. Yes, I agree
we can try to work out the risks of the tasks we can see but we can not

establish the risk of activities which are going to turn up out of the blue and surprise us.

Unexpected Perspectives.

For this I always suggest posting a look-out on a hill to spot the enemy army on the horizon marching in to launch a surprise attack on us. At least one core team member should have the job of studying the world outside of the project, to look for any changes in the big picture (see Section 2.2.2. Establishing Hard and Soft Criteria).

Perspectives on Tasks

Not all tasks that you can see have the same need for your attention. Some are not only risky but can cause overall project failure. The trick here is to segment your key tasks on the grid below. Go back to your sticky steps and transfer the step numbers into the appropriate quadrant.

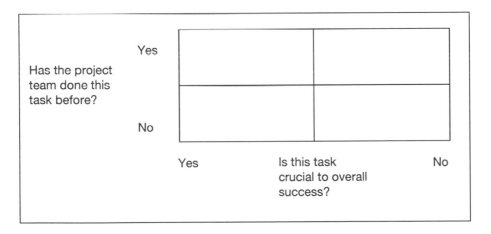

Fig. 2.20 Perspectives on tasks – finding potential risk

Your question now must be 'and so what do I do about this?' I recommend the strategies below.

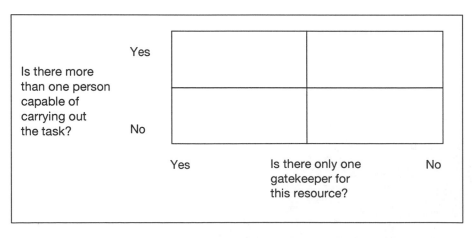

		Yes	Pay attention to these. You can delegate these to core team members.	Pay attention to these before each time buffer.

Has the project team done this task before?

| | No | Stay close to these. Check on these very frequently. | Pay attention to these only if they start to get late |

Yes   Is this task crucial to overall success?   No

Fig. 2.21 Perspectives on tasks – what to do about it

Now transfer the tasks in the bottom left hand quadrant to the grid below.

Yes

Is there more than one person capable of carrying out the task?

No

Yes   Is there only one gatekeeper for this resource?   No

Fig. 2.22 Perspectives on tasks – finding potential resource risk

192

Actions to be tasked are outlined below.

Is there more than one person capable of carrying out the task?	Yes	Build credits with possible backup. Add their name to your stakeholder map	No immediate strategy needed.
	No	Build a robust relationship with this person. Draw a box around their name on your stakeholder map	Build credits with another gatekeeper. Add their name to your stakeholder map.
		Yes	Is there only one gatekeeper for this resource? No

Fig. 2.23 Perspectives on tasks – what to do about it

INDIVIDUAL TAILORING

Painting-by-numbers: *Be especially careful of the risks to completion posed by shared or common resources. Schedule these first and then try to fit all your other tasks around them. Place milestones at the point of handover to a critical shared resource and at the point of completion.*

Invisible projects: *You will need to invent 'dummy variables' to monitor, almost anything will do from culture surveys to lines of code.*

Walking in the Fog projects: *These are naturally very risky. Monitor resource use and money spend carefully to make sure that it is still worth trying to get out of the fog.*

CommErcial projects: *Make sure that any particularly risky tasks are placed after staged payments. This will guarantee your cash flows whilst allowing you the time to handle the risks posed.*

Section 2.3.4
Communications Strategies

If you wish to converse with me, define your terms.
Voltaire

You need to establish two strategies. One for **sending out** your messages in order to keep your stakeholders in balance and to ensure that tasks are carried out as required. The second to make sure that you **collect all the information** you need to keep the project co-ordinated and on track.

COMMUNICATING OUT

Naming change

Change doesn't really come to life until it has a name. Once it has a name it is possible to talk about the chunk as a real discrete entity. It's true that 'a rose by any other name would smell as sweet'. <u>You</u> have the rose. <u>You</u> can smell it. When managing change in chunks, you're not even sure if what <u>you</u> are after is a flower. It could be a bottle of perfume or a brightly coloured piece of tissue paper.

> The first project I ever had to name was a research project I was leading for an oil company. The project was a quest to remove poisonous and corrosive sulphur products from North Sea gases. There had been many attempts to tackle this quest. My attempt was based on the ability of some very weird bacteria called *Thiobacillus Ferrooxidans*, to live on this foul and poisonous diet. We ended up calling the project the T-Fox (pronounced Teefox) project. The name was rapidly assimilated amongst my co-workers and seemed to encapsulate the project concept. It kept us focused on the aims of the project and the bigger picture.

Project names are a very important way of encapsulating the project concept, that idea behind the project.

How do I select a suitable name?

- Making a Movie: A description of the what e.g. Rocky 4, Info Retrieve, Eurodrive for a pan-European sales initiative.
- Going on a Quest: A description of the how e.g. Link-Up for a business re-engineering project.
- Fog walking: Name relating to a current vision or past vision or past visionary e.g. Horizon, Rubicon, Gallileo.
- Painting-by-numbers: Name is less critical. May relate to original

masterpiece; changes or improvements to what or how the masterpiece is being reproduced or a number or code.

LEVERAGE FOR BALANCING STAKEHOLDERS

You can raise or lower expectations at any time and in any way but there are times of best leverage.

- Manage the point of access, the point of impact (see Section 2.2.4 Balancing Stakeholder Expectations, for explanation), set milestones during the delivery so that you can go back and check how their expectations are being met.
- Remember, when you are most busy your stakeholders are usually most idle and susceptible. It is important that you communicate when you are most busy. For this you will need to enlist help or use a system. Your team or secretary can help. The basic message you want them to receive is that '. . . is going well' and that you have '. . . not forgotten them'. (I also make use of standard pre-written letters.)
- Always alert stakeholders to any change in plans as early as possible.

It is usually most effective to give bad news in two shots.

I have some very bad news
The bad news is . . .

or

You are going to be very unhappy with me.
You remember the date I promised for hand over? Well, I'm not going to make it.

INSTRUCTING TASKS

Generally, in change situations instructions which are issued are being issued for the **first** and possibly **only** time, so it is essential that the person receiving the instruction works their way round the learning cycle (see Section 2.1. Learning to Learn).

Communicating Out: Instructions

In issuing instructions make sure that you outline in order:

THE PROBLEM/ISSUE/UPDATE	The market research is late.
THE IMPACT ON BIG PICTURE	This means that we can not start work on the advertising brief.

NOW DESCRIBE THE PROBLEM AT THE RIGHT LEVEL (SEE CHAPTER FOUR)	The tables at the back will need to have the demographic details changed.
THE OWNERSHIP OF THE TASK (SEE CHAPTER NINE)	I would like you to help with this.
PAUSE (OR ASK FOR HELP OR IDEAS OR ADVICE DEPENDING ON SITUATION) (SEE CHAPTER EIGHT)	What could you do?
AND IF APPROPRIATE	
WHAT HAS TO BE DONE AND/OR HOW IT HAS TO BE DONE	OK, so you will chase them up by 'phone, but be hard on them.

What is the key question you must ask at the end of each instruction? No, it is not, 'Do you understand?' People usually say 'Yes' to that. They don't know that they don't understand. Instead you ask, **'What are the implications for you?'** or **'What does this mean you will have to do?'**

CHECK THAT THEY HAVE BEEN ROUND THE LEARNING CYCLE	'What are the implications for you?

The only way that someone can answer that is to work their way round the learning cycle. Your instruction is the *experience*. They then need to *reflect* on it and then work out a *general theory* of how they think it will affect them and then tell you what they intend to do as a *test*.

Communicating Out: Scheduling

In Section 2.2.4 Maintaining Balance, page 168, you segmented your stakeholders into three categories. Now you will need to decide when to schedule communication with them.

WHEN SHOULD I COMMUNICATE WITH THEM. SHOULD IT BE REGULAR/ SCHEDULED OR AD HOC? A USEFUL PATTERN IS:

WORK ON PROJECT WITH STAKE HOLDERS WHO HAVE AN INTEREST DURING . . . REINFORCE ABSOLUTELY CRITICAL STAKEHOLDERS . . . WORK ON PROJECT . . . CHECK WITH STAKEHOLDERS INTERESTED IN OUTCOME . . . WORK ON PROJECT . . . REINFORCE ABSOLUTELY CRITICAL STAKEHOLDERS . . . WORK ON PROJECT . . . CLEAR CHANNELS TO DIVERT STAKEHOLDERS THE PROJECT CAN 'HAPPEN WITHOUT' . . . WORK ON PROJECT . . . REINFORCE ABSOLUTELY CRITICAL STAKEHOLDERS . . . WORK ON PROJECT.

WHAT IS THE MOST APPROPRIATE METHOD? LETTER, PHONE, FAX? (CHECK SOFT CRITERIA.)

MUST I DO ALL OF IT MYSELF OR CAN A TEAM MEMBER HELP?

Communicating In

Have you ever received a progress report which has left you bewildered? The type with rows and columns of meaningless figures, or a long list of tasks? How can you co-ordinate activities on the basis of such a report? How does this happen? I think it is because the process of communicating in has not been thought out.

As leader you want to know certain things. In order to maintain co-ordination during the change what do you need to know? You will need to find out about both stakeholders and tasks. The level and frequency of co-ordination is dependent on the type of project (see individual tailoring below, and on the rate of learning required by the change (see Section 2.1.3 Review Management).

You need information and not data. *Information is the answer to a specifically asked question.* You will therefore have to decide most of your questions in advance to make sure that the appropriate data has been collected. Your questions will need to address both the hard and soft criteria of the project.

Go back to the Big Picture (Section 2.2.2, page 148). Remind yourself of the hard and soft criteria.

ASK YOURSELF:

- HOW WILL I KNOW IF I AM MAKING PROGRESS?
- WHO IS THE BEST PERSON TO SAY?
- HOW SHOULD I GET THEM TO TELL ME? (FREQUENCY/LEVEL OF COMMUNICATION)
- HOW DO I GET THEM TO REALISE THAT IT IS IMPORTANT THAT I KNOW THE PROGRESS OF THE PROJECT?

INDIVIDUAL TAILORING

Invisible projects: *You must be like a mime artist, make the invisible seem visible. Use anything at your disposal. Workshops, memos, presentations, tables of what I call 'dummy variables': these are arbitary variables, such as lines of code, or staff attitude indices, written whilst meaning little, they appear to make progress visible. Naming is a very effective way of raising visibility. Have a project naming competition – name and brand. Make your own letter-headed paper to use for all internal communication. Always refer to the project name in conversations as if it were a person. Never use the words project, programme or initiative, only use the name on it's own.*

CommErcial projects: *Deciding on a name with the client is a very effective method of building links between the internal and external stakeholders. Unfortunately, external projects tend to be closed and do not need specific names. Referring to projects internally by the client's name works for the internal team but is useless to the external client.*

Joint Ventures: *Try to select a name which does not reflect the parent companies' interests. In this way, the joint venture can be felt to be a stand alone entity, rather than a small, less siginficant offshoot. This will usually be difficult, since there are usually political reasons for the joint venture. This means that the parent organisations will wish to have the origins of the joint venture in the name. If this is the case include their names as a by-line.*

Section 2.4
WORKING WITH AND LEADING PEOPLE

We will either find a way or we will make a way.
Hannibal

So what is this thing of working with others to create something new. To create something which none of us could create on our own. To create something which is often more than the sum of the parts? Surely that's what organisations do. But somehow I do not see many advertisements for leader of function, general leader, senior leader, corporate leader, leading director, chief executive leader, shop floor leader, finance leader. I do see advertisements for head of function, general manager, senior manager, corporate executive, managing director, chief executive officer, shop floor supervisor, and finance manager. Is it purely semantics? Just words, or is there a meaning behind the words?

I think that there is meaning. And I think that there is a different meaning to *leader* and *manager*. And that there is a need for **different types of leadership in different types of change**. This means that there are actually fewer common threads in this chapter. So unlike other chapters, this chapter will separately address the different ways of leading the four main types of change. The section on individual tailoring will address only Visibility and Drive (see Section 1.2. What type is it?).

HOW DO YOU WORK WITH AND LEAD PEOPLE?

A FIRST QUIZ

For each of the statements below select three endings that best describe *you* when you are working with others.

Assign five (5) points to the ending that best describes you, three (3) points to the second and one (1) to the ending ranked third.

When I have to work with others I feel most comfortable if I am
a. The expert. ☐
b. Helping them get along. ☐
c. Figuring out ways to do things. ☐
d. Getting on with the work. ☐
e. Making sure that everyone knows what to do ☐

a__b__c__d__e__

When I have to work with others I feel happiest if I am
a. The only person who has done it before.   ☐
b. Adding to team cohesiveness and morale.   ☐
c. Sorting out how we can get help.   ☐
d. Making sure that we make progress.   ☐
e. Checking that we are going to produce a high
    quality result.   ☐

a___b___c___d___e___

When I have to work with others I feel most confident if I can
a. use experience I have gained from the past.   ☐
b. Be allowed to contribute to what others are
    doing.   ☐
c. Suggest where we can get additional help.   ☐
d. Be sure that we are pushing towards success.   ☐
e. Tell that we are approaching the change in a
    considered and practical manner.   ☐

a___b___c___d___e___

When I have to work with others I like to think that I can
a. Provide the right answers.   ☐
b. Keep people feeling part of the team.   ☐
c. Come up with creative ways of solving problems. ☐
d. Make sure that all the loose ends are tied up.   ☐
e. Be counted on to involve all members of the
    team.   ☐

a___b___c___d___e___

When I have to work with others I see myself as
a. The person who can tell others what to do.   ☐
b. The diplomat.   ☐
c. The fixer.   ☐
d. The person who is happy working.   ☐
e. The person whom other people can approach.   ☐

a___b___c___d___e___

I am most likely to say,
a. 'That's not how it's done.'   ☐
b. 'Tell me how I can help.'   ☐
c. 'I have got an idea.'   ☐
d. 'I took it home and finished it off.'   ☐
e. 'I don't think that we are going to be ready on
    time.'   ☐

a___b___c___d___e___

I am most likely to say,
a. 'I told them it would never work.' ☐
b. 'Is everybody happy?' ☐
c. 'I know a man who can.' ☐
d. 'J.F.D.I.! (Just Do It!)' ☐
e. 'Does everyone know what they have to do
   next?' ☐

a__b__c__d__e__

I am most likely to say,
a. 'What do they know about it? ☐
b. 'I'm not sure I understand what this means.' ☐
c. 'Why don't we do it this way?' ☐
d. 'I'll do it.' ☐
e. 'Wait a second. We've not heard what Anne
   thinks.' ☐

a__b__c__d__e__

Scoring

Just add up the totals for each question letter. (Overall total should be 72)

a_____   b_____   c_____   d_____   e_____
KN_____   CA_____   SO_____   DO_____   CH_____

A SECOND QUIZ

For each pair of answers please tick the **one** that best answers the question for *you*.

When I am responsible for delivering change, I feel more comfortable if I am
a. The most experienced. ☐
b. Challenging others to think and do new things. ☐

a__b__c__d__e__f__

When I am responsible for delivering change, I feel more comfortable if I am
c. Having to spend time to make sure that I
   understand how I can use my skills to achieve the
   objective. ☐
d. Getting on with the work. ☐

a__b__c__d__e__f__

When I am responsible for delivering change, I feel more comfortable if I am
e. Exploring several alternative routes. ☐

201

f. Finding out with my team what is expected of us. ☐

a__b__c__d__e__f__

When I have been asked to deliver change I feel happiest if I am
a. Left with clear objectives and methodology to get
    on with it. ☐
b. Allowed to change and redefine the needs myself,
    as I see them. ☐

a__b__c__d__e__f__

When I have been asked to deliver change I feel happiest if I am
d. Given clear accountabilities and responsibilities. ☐
e. Allowed to find my own routes to deliver the
    specified deliverables. ☐

a__b__c__d__e__f__

When I have been asked to deliver change I feel happiest if I am
c. Allowed to comment on the deliverables and
    suggest alternatives based on our methods. ☐
f. Not constrained to specific detailed deliverables
    as long as I produce something of value. ☐

a__b__c__d__e__f__

When I have to manage a project I feel most confident if I can
a. Use experience I have gained from the past. ☐
b. Be given a decent sized budget and access to
    resources and left to get on. ☐

a__b__c__d__e__f__

When I have to manage a project I feel most confident if I can
f. Choose to work with people I respect who are
    creative and communicative. ☐
d. Choose to work with people who are experienced
    and professional. ☐

a__b__c__d__e__f__

When I have to manage a project I feel most confident if I can
c. Choose a wide range of different people to help
    me work out what I should be doing. ☐
e. Choose to work with people who are dedicated
    and single minded. ☐

a__b__c__d__e__f__

When it's down to me to get others to work on a project, I like to think that I can
a. Provide the right answers to my team and other stakeholders. ☐
b. Provide the intellectual challenge to others to make them come up with the best answers. ☐

a_b_c_d_e_f_

When it's down to me to get others to work on a project, I like to think that I can
c. Make sure that people are asking the right questions. ☐
f. Make sure that people are trying to understand what is happening around them. ☐

a_b_c_d_e_f_

When it's down to me to get others to work on a project, I like to think that I can
e. Check the answers people are coming up with. ☐
d. Make sure that people are searching for the right answers. ☐

a_b_c_d_e_f_

When I have to work with others I see myself as
a. The person who is making sure that we do it better this time than we did last time. ☐
b. The person who is making sure that we do it differently this time than we did last time. ☐

a_b_c_d_e_f_

When I have to work with others I see myself as
c. The person who makes sure we apply all our skills and knowledge to the problem at hand. ☐
e. The person who makes sure that we invent new ways of doing things. ☐

a_b_c_d_e_f_

When I have to work with others I see myself as
f. The person who can come up with ways of progressing if we get stuck. ☐
d. The person who can be relied upon to give clear instructions and guidance. ☐

a_b_c_d_e_f_

I am more likely to say,
a. 'How are we doing according to the plan?' ☐
b. 'How about if we try this?' ☐

a_b_c_d_e_f_

203

I am more likely to say,
d. 'I've been thinking about this for some time.'   ☐
e. 'It would be really great if. . .'   ☐

a__b__c__d__e__f__

I am more likely to say,
c. 'I think we will do a better job this time.'   ☐
f. I think that we are going to have to experiment.'   ☐

a__b__c__d__e__f__

I am more likely to say,
a. 'I prefer evolutionary change.'   ☐
b. 'I prefer revolutionary change.'   ☐

a__b__c__d__e__f__

I am more likely to say,
c. 'Let's spend some more time working out
    precisely what we should be aiming at.'   ☐
d. 'J.F.D.I.! (Just Do It!)'   ☐

a__b__c__d__e__f__

I am more likely to say,
e. 'At least we now know how not to do it.'   ☐
f. 'One step at a time.'   ☐

a__b__c__d__e__f__

Others see me as
a. A person who conforms.   ☐
b. A person who is happy to change a plan at a
    moment's notice.   ☐

a__b__c__d__e__f__

Others see me as
d. Measured systematic and methodical.   ☐
e. Often seduced by a cause.   ☐

a__b__c__d__e__f__

Others see me as
a. Capable in my area of knowledge and skills.   ☐
f. Needing the stimulation of constant change.   ☐

a__b__c__d__e__f__

Scoring

Please calculate the number of ticks for each letter answer. (The total should come to 24.)

a____ b____ c____ d____ e____ f____

Section 2.4.1
Leadership? What leadership?

A man runs into the room naked, painted blue and proclaiming the end of the world. If he's on his own, he's escaped from the local asylum, if there are fifty others running behind him, doing the same thing, he's a leader.
Jim Durcan

By now, millons of softwood trees will have been chopped down to provide the paper pulp for books on leadership. What, you must be thinking, can this handbook add? The answer, I hope, is levers. The few little things which you, as a leader, can do when managing different types of change, and which have a tremendous impact.

For me, the quotation at the start of this section explains it to me. The secret of leadership is in the word itself. A person who is devoted to being a vehicle to follow. Leaders are defined not by the organisation, not by themselves, but by the people who follow. The issue is **how do I get people to follow me?**

In a project or change situation this is particularly important. In modern projects it is unusual for the person leading a chunk of change to have complete power, in a formal or informal sense, over all the project stakeholders. Often they may have formal power over some core team members. In modern projects, it is unusual for the project leader to have full responsibility or full control over the actions of their stakeholders; and yet the project leader continues to be held fully accountable for project success by *all* the stakeholders. If the project fails in any way all fingers point at the project leader. And a very short time after the change starts the project leader has a fuller understanding of the change than anyone else. The only way to get the project to an acceptable point is to get **all** the stakeholders to **follow** the project **leader**.

In the next few sections, I intend to approach the subject of leadership in an unconventional way – the wrong way. Each time, I intend to look at the issues from the other person's point of view. From the point of view of the follower.

FOLLOW THE LEADER

PAINTING-BY-NUMBERS

Towards the end of a week's skiing, all the pistes in the resort have been skied several times. It is common for good skiers to look for opportunities for skiing away from the safe, neatly marked tracks. There is the call of fresh virgin snow, the desire to ski 'off piste'. This practice of off piste skiing covers anything from setting off down the wrong side of the mountain (for wimps), to hiring a helicopter to take you to a distant peak and then to leave you there to find your own way back. Skiing off piste is really only open to those who have mastered skiing. Those who know what to do and how to do it in both simple and tricky situations. Nevertheless, the people who are still alive after the experience of real 'off piste' skiing tend to be those wise enough to employ a guide. In theory, the guide is someone with a good local knowledge of the area. Someone who can keep you away from murderous crevices, knows where the best snow is to be found. Someone to follow on this exciting but dangerous trip.

But how do you select a guide? What do you look for? For a start a guide must be steadfast and true or how can he be called a guide? Must look as if they were born with skis already attached to their feet. Must have done it before several times (this is what is known as a 'piste' record). Must be able to issue orders in a language you understand so that you will be well instructed at the critical times. And must look as if they are the sort of person you would follow and obey in a crisis or when things are going well.

You follow them because of what they offer you; experience, knowledge, certainty, excitement at such a difficult and demanding task. Or you follow them because of what they can deny you. They know the score better than you so they can punish, frighten, or bully you. They trade with you. Perform and I reward you – don't perform and I punish you.

GOING ON A QUEST

I have a friend who once recounted this story. In the late sixties he got a job to study the molecular structures of Soy proteins. At the time both the Green movement and Vegetarianism were gaining momentum and there was a need to develop meat substitutes. Soy beans were the natural choice, being high in protein. But once cooked, they smelt and tasted like beans and not like meat. Housewives would only buy meat substitutes which you could cook like meat – say in casseroles – and smelt and tasted like meat. It was a challenge. No one at the time had a clue how to heat-treat vegetable proteins in order to get them to look and feel like animal protein. If only they could get meat substitutes to taste and feel like meat, there would be millions to be made.

But how do you select a King? How do you select a zealot? What do you look for? For a start a King must embody the needs of the quest or the quest itself. For example, King Arthur was actually ill and it was felt that the Holy Grail would revive both him and the lands of England. Edison is reputed to have tried thousands of different combinations and formulations of metals before finally finding one which would allow his invention, the light bulb, to work. His desire for illumination matched the illumination promised by the outcome of the quest. A zealot must be zealous or how can he be called a zealot?

A leader of a quest must give life to the already seductive idea. Must look as if they were born with this one single goal. Must appear to have an unbreakable pact with God. Must be a 'person of destiny'. Must be able to articulate *the cause*, an already seductive argument and make you believe that, more than anything else you also want this challenge to be met and overcome. Must be able to make you feel that 'it would be nice if. . .' or 'if only . . . all would be well'.

You follow them because of the cause. Because of how they embody it. What they offer you is challenge, adventure, discovery, the opportunity to work with people of a like mind and at the end, an outcome such as mankind has never before seen. Or you follow them because of fear of falling out with the other believers. You may follow because of guilt at having let the cause down. Guilt about your co-workers or fear of loneliness at the loss of comradeship or compansionship.

WALKING IN THE FOG

The first full wedding in a family is often a trying time. All the family and friends are unsure of exactly how to get things going. They know there is to be a wedding but are unsure of exactly what this entails. They are also uncertain of how to go about planning and organising and each has their own vision of what the day should be like. Each tries to create the vision in their own mind. Since each has a slighly different vision, tensions and stresses start to arise. Unless a clear leader emerges and leads the stakeholders, the bride and groom find themselves caught in a pan-dimensional tussle for leadership. Even if a leader does emerge, it is absolutely essential that everyone follows the leader or else what should be the couple's happiest day turns out to be the start of a lifelong, inter-family or intra-family feud. The successful leader keeps everyone up to date, welcomes inputs and suggests and realigns them with the overall vision.

But how do you select a visionary? What do you look for? After all you could make your own way in the fog. A leader in the fog must seem to have a compass in their head. For a start a visionary must have a vision. But what is a vision? I think that a vision is a picture which the visionary can see clearly in their mind's eye. A picture of a possible future. A picture that conjures up reactions in you. Reactions in you which are both logical and emotional. The vision that they describe to you must be clear and unwavering, otherwise it could just be a mirage. They must tell it to you like a fairy tale. Paint pictures with words. And just like telling kids a fairy tale they may add detail to the vision but they may not leave bits out.

The visionary must seem to have as much to lose by not leading you out of the fog as you do. Must be able to give you hope when it seems impossible that you will find your way out. Must act out the vision and be a role model so that you can see it alive, embodied and be able to copy or reproduce it. Must challenge and praise. Must appear to care personally about you as an individual. Must take from you offerings, ideas and efforts which lead towards the vision.

You follow them because of how they are, how they behave and the vision that they offer which you do not have but could share. What they offer you is an opportunity to stretch yourself into areas you have never been. An opportunity to invent, to create, to live, to travel a magical mystery tour.

MAKING A MOVIE

A shipbuilding company which specialised in hand-building wooden luxury yachts had been steadily losing money for two years. Little that the management did had any effect. They were unable to generate more sales. Eventually the Chief Executive and two other directors got the sack. But rather than replace them with appointments from the inside, the board insisted on bringing in an outsider. The staff were dismayed. Most of them had spent their lives learning the skills that they applied to shipbuilding. The outsider was to be a twenty-nine year old who had never worked in shipbuilding before. The new Boss wasted little time looking for further orders for ships. Instead he held a brainstorming session to see 'What else we could do with our skills?

The staff were sceptical but he explained to them that there would be opportunities to use their skills in other ways. In the end they moved from shipbuilding into manufacturing designer furniture.

But how do you select a Producer/Director? What do you look for? For a start a producer/director must be committed. Must manage the outside world for you in order to allow you to concentrate on your contribution. Must set the highest professional standards for you and must give you the chance to use your personal skills or resources to the fullest.

You follow them becauuse of what they offer you – experience that allows them to know what they are looking for when they see it. You follow for their previous style, knowledge, the certainty that they will be able to pull together unrelated strands into a cohesive and meaningful whole. You follow them because they allow you to demonstrate your skills to the fullest.

Section 2.4.2
Lead the followers

If you want to become a leader, find a parade and get in front of it!
Snoopy the Dog

Now we need to look at the followers from the point of view of the leader. What is the leader looking for in followers? I think we need to split them into two groups, the core team, who will be central to the change and may end up having to lead other stakeholders themselves, and all the other stakeholders.

HOW ABOUT THE CORE TEAM?

What is a team? Is a team simply a fancy word for a group of people? What is the difference between a team and a task force? What is the difference between a team and a committee? Is a team simply a group of people with different skills aiming for the same goal? If it is why do soccer clubs with talented players who are good individual players often not perform as well as teams with a wider spread of abilities, and even stand accused of not playing as a team? I think that a team is something different. I think that teams only occur when **a number of people** have a **common goal** and **recognise** that their **personal success** is dependent on the success of others. That is, they are all **interdependent**. What does this mean? It means that in most teams, people will contribute individual skills, many of which will be different. It also means that the full tensions and counter balance of human behaviours will need to be demonstrated in the team.

As in the soccer example, it is not enough to have the individual skills. You need players' behaviours to mesh together in order to achieve greatness. You need someone to pass the ball, even when they have a good chance of scoring, to another with a better chance. You need someone to work out and share the best tactics for getting the ball past the opponents' defence and so on.

As leader you will either have your team given to you or you will have the chance of selecting and assembling them yourself. How do you know if you have the right mix? How do you know if they will gel and become a high performing team?

For people to work well together you need **both** a range of **specific or technical skills** and a range of **different human behaviours.** When you look hard at people and how they behave when they are working in teams you find that in addition to the actual content of the work they are doing,

210

they take on certain behaviours. Each person has favourite ways of behaving when they work with others. Usually their favourite ways are the ways of behaving with which they feel most comfortable.

I'd like you to look at human behaviour interactions. I think that for people to work in teams you need them behaving in certain ways. You need some people to concentrate on the task at hand (**Doers**). You need some people to provide specialist knowledge (**Knowers**) and some to solve problems as they arise (**Solvers**). You need some people to make sure that it is going as well as it can and that the whole team is contributing fully (**Checkers**). And you need some people to make sure that the team is operating as a cohesive social unit (**Carers**).

Is this roughly right?

Some of you may be familiar with a model of team roles which breaks team behaviour into nine rather than five roles. I find nine roles a bit too many to remember but I have created a conversion chart, a bit like the sort of chart you would use for converting gallons to litres, for you to use.

Solver: Plant and resource investigator behaviours.
Doer: Shaper, Implementer and Completer Finisher behaviours.
Checker: Co-ordinator, Monitor Evaluator.
Carer: Teamworker.
Knower: Specialist.
(See References *Management Teams* R. M. Belbin)

BALANCED TEAMS?

Modern management thinking suggests that you need a *balance* of behaviours for any change management activity. I think it is a bit more complex than that. I think that once you have really understood human behaviours in teams, you may wish to slightly unbalance the team in favour of the type of change you are trying to undertake.

Painting-by-Numbers

But how do you select a team? How do you select the people you want to follow you? What is the best mix? Generally if you are Painting-by-Numbers as a leader you want to do a more complex or closely specified project to a higher quality, faster or to complete bang on time, cheaper or with better financial returns. You need high quality specialist professionals. Being specialists they will not necessarily have much respect for each other's contributions. So points of hand over (painting up to the line) will have to be dealt with carefully. What you want is for them to have such

HUMAN BEHAVIOURS

Description	Behaviour in team	Tasks performed
Solver	Helps team to solve problems by coming up with ideas or by finding resources from outside the team. Can see another way forward.	Provides innovation, imagination & unorthodoxy. Good networker. Develops contacts. Negotiates for resources. Develops and generates ideas.
Doer	Concentrates on the task: getting it started, keeping it going, getting it done or making sure it is finished. Some behaviours may focus only one phase of the task. Making sure it's finished is most rare.	Provides energy or motivation. Pushes others into action. Practical implementation. Ensures a systematic approach. Follows through. Gives attention to detail.
Checker	Concern for the whole process. Tries to ensure full participation whilst providing a balanced view of quality and time and realism.	Suggests reflection. Thinks critically. Provides shrewd judgements. Makes others work towards shared goals. Makes use of individual talents. Makes sure resources are fully used.
Carer	Concern for the individuals in the team and how they are developing and getting along.	Provides personal support. Shows concern for others. Gives flexibility to help out. Creates the social system.
Knower	Provider of specialist knowledge or experience	Provides standards and focus

an overpowering desire to perform their parts as a team that they will actually work together and support each other in order to get the work done.

You unbalance in favour of knowers and checkers.

Going on a Quest

But how do you select a team? How do you select the people you want to follow you? What is the best mix? Generally if you are Going on a Quest you need knights. You need self-reliant people with a passion for the quest who will leave no stone unturned in the adventure of the quest. People who, without hesitation, will rally to each other's calls and provide support in tricky situations. Focus on making sure that your team involves doers and solvers. It may be worth unbalancing your team in this direction.

You unbalance in favour of doers and solvers.

Walking in the Fog

But how do you select a team? How do you select the people you want to follow you? What is the best mix? Generally if you are Walking in the Fog you need people who are keen to take a step into the fog. You do not want people who wish to sit down and wait until the fog clears until they do something. People must be willing and able to be intellectually challenged and learn. And they must be keen on holding hands, sharing ideas and communicating. You want a wide range of skills, although the individual's actual skill levels are not paramount nor as critical as they are if you are Painting-by-Numbers. You want a full balance of behaviours. That way there is always a creative and achievement based tension in the team which allows it to tackle the change as it emerges. If you are missing any of the behaviours described above, especially solver or carers, your team is unlikely to make good progress in this type of project. A lack of carers will mean that the tensions are resolved destructively rather than con-structively.

You unbalance slightly away from knowers and slightly in favour of solvers and carers.

Making a Movie

But how do you select a team? How do you select the people you want to follow you? What is the best mix? Generally if you are Making a Movie you need on your team people who will be able to contribute both to finding the right script and to the actual filming. You want a wide mix of skills. You may not want all at once. You want a wide range of behaviors with an

213

emphasis on solvers for the first part of the change and an emphasis on knowers for the second stage.

You balance in favour of knowers and solvers.

HOW ABOUT OTHER STAKEHOLDERS?

Other stakeholders have their own individual reasons for following you. If you have spent time establishing their values (see Section 2.2.2. Establishing Hard and Soft Criteria), you will need to think through why they would follow you for each case, especially the driver stakeholders. For closed projects you can get them to follow you by trading, whereas with open projects all you can offer are visions and challenge.

You may wish to skew this if a stakeholder's soft criteria suggests that they are unhappy with uncertainty and the project is open. In this case lower the profile of the more open aspects whilst raising the profile of any achieved tasks. This will help them to follow you and will help the progress of the project.

You will need to spend some time establishing who your invisible team are and how best to get them to follow you. Most commonly people use an adaptive leadership approach. Before the project starts they spend time using the known business environment to build up favours and credits. These can then be called up during the project.

Section 2.4.3
Matching the Person To the Chunk

I contradict myself. I am large. I contain multitudes.
Walt Whitman

WHAT DOES THIS MEAN FOR ME?

The two quizzes at the start of the section should have helped establish how you contribute when you are working with others and which types of projects you will feel most comfortable with leading. They establish *preferences* not *personality*. You visit someone and they ask 'Coffee or tea?' Most times you go for coffee. It doesn't mean you don't drink tea; it just means that coffee is your preference. A preference is just a personal foible.

HOW YOU PREFER TO CONTRIBUTE TO A TEAM

Step 1 Transfer your results from Quiz 1 in Section 2.4 page 00
        KN_____   CA_____   SO_____   DO_____   CH_____

Step 2 Multiply all the scores by 100
        KN_____   CA_____   SO_____   DO_____   CH_____

Step 3 Divide all the scores in Step 2 by the highest score from Step 1. (One score must read 100, ignore fractions; round the numbers up.)
        KN_____   CA_____   SO_____   DO_____   CH_____

Step 4 Circle the categories of behaviour below which score more than 50 in Step 3.
        KNOWER   CARER   SOLVER   DOER   CHECKER

A score of 100 is your favourite way of contributing to teams.
A score of 75 to 100 is a close second. You often use this behaviour.
A score of 50 to 75 is a behaviour you sometimes use.
A score of less than 50 is one you rarely ever use.

WHAT TYPES OF CHANGE DO YOU PREFER TO LEAD?

Step 1 Please transfer your scores from Quiz 1 in Section 2.4, page 199.
        a____   b____   c____   d____   e____   f____   (total = 24)

Step 2 Transfer scores:

b	b	a	a
+ e	+ f	+ c	+ d
− c	− a	− e	− b
	− d		− f

Totals _____   _____   _____   _____

Step 3 Please circle the largest score

PIONEER   INNOVATOR   CRAFTSMAN   ADAPTER

In general, the preferred types of change people like to lead are:

- **Pioneers** feel most comfortable with Going on **Quests**
- **Innovators** feel most comfortable with Walking in the **Fog**
- **Craftsmen** feel most comfortable with Making a **Movie**
- **Adaptors** feel most comfortable with **Painting-by-Numbers**

The task for you is now to establish what impact your particular style and way of working with others impacts on your role as a leader. For example, how do you think an *Adapter* asked to walk in the *fog* who tends to act as a *knower* in a team would behave? This is a nice easy example. They would look for something in their own personal area of expertise which they could address, focus the whole project and team on that. They would ignore the bigger picture and push people to achieve the narrowly defined aim. Apart from members of the team who were doers or knowers in the same specialism, their team would **not** follow them. Even worse, the team would look on them with scorn and poke fun at them. Humour of the 'If all you have is a hammer then everything looks like a nail!' variety would abound. Other stakeholders would find that their broader expectations were not being met and the project would fail.

NOW IT'S YOUR TURN

My approach to change is: _____

I contribute to teams as: _____

My chunk of change is: _____   (See Section 1.3 What sort of problems should you expect? Do you
remember crystal ball gazing?)

_____

_____

_____

_____

_____

_____

_____

_____

_____

INDIVIDUAL TAILORING

Invisible projects: *If you are leading an invisible project, beware if you are an innovator. Innovators are often introverts. You will need to be extrovert because in order to get people to follow you and in order to be a role model to your team you will need to be visible, you will need to be seen doing things. If you are leading an invisible quest or fog project you will need to regularly rally your followers, reminding them of how much you have done and how much ground you have covered.*

Section 2.4.4
A Last Word

When all has been said and done . . . a lot more has been said than done.
Anon

Managing all change is demanding. Manage it in chunks or as projects. You will need to learn facts, skills and behaviours which you have never needed before. You will need to learn to recognise types of change and learn how to lead other people through an ever changing world. I hope that in some way this handbook has helped you understand how to make a difference. Please don't keep it secret, share it with a colleague, spouse or friend.

Let me know how you get on. There is an address at the end of the book.

Good luck.

Part 3
ALL THOSE NEW WORDS

If you use a word a man can't understand, why, you might just as well insult him.
John Steinbeck

HOW TO USE THIS GLOSSARY

This glossary contains a whole range of terms associated with *All Change*. I have tried to avoid using jargon when giving explanations, however this is not always possible. I have therefore highlighted all terms which need further explanation. The explanations are provided elsewhere in the glossary.

Section 3.1
THE EXPLANATIONS

Big Picture   The big picture gives the context for the project. It is best understood by asking the question 'Why do they want it?' for each stakeholder grouping. The answer to this question will usually include reasons which relate to the strategic and commercial environment, those which relate to organisation structure and politics, and some reasons which relate to personal ambitions.

Change Projects   These are internal projects. They are driven by the organisation which has to change.

Client   Client is a loosely defined term and refers to one or more people in the **client organisation**.

Client Organisation   The client organisation wants to use the output from the project. Specific people in the client organisation include the **key contact**, the **client sponsor** and the **end user**. This is usually the organisation which **drives** the change.

The client organisation can be completely separate from the **project organisation**. For example the client organisation is the company which commissions an advertising campaign from an advertising agency. Alternatively, it can be a separate department or division within the project organisation. For example when the Human Resources Department is asked to implement a new performance related pay scheme in the Operations Division, Operations Division is the client.

Client Sponsor   The client is the person in the **client organisation** who wants the project completed. The relationship between the **client sponsor** and the **key contact** mirrors the relationship between the **sponsor** and the **project leader** in the **project organisation**. Occasionally the **client sponsor** and the **key contact** are the same person.

Closed Projects   Closed projects have clear goals and a clearly defined set of activities to be carried out, they are characterised by the phrase 'we will know when we have completed the clearly defined deliverable'. Examples include building a bridge or launching a clearly specified new product.

Colloquially described as **painting-by-numbers**.

Collaborative Project   See Joint Venture.

Core Team   In projects where there is a large **visible team** there is usually a sub group of five to ten visible team members who act as the core team. This core team works with the **project leader** and takes the operational decisions relating to the project.

Commercial Projects   These are projects run to make money directly from the project itself. Money is made by the organisation **delivering** the project.

Contract Project   This sort of project is **internally driven** and **externally delivered**. Your organisation pays another organisation to deliver a service.

Directional Strategy   A directional strategy is a statement of 'where we want to go'. It has clear goals and the way forward is clear. There is little uncertainty, so forward planning is appropriate.

Drive (Driven, Drivers)   Drivers are the people who demand and define change. Drive is the role of the **sponsor, client** and **end user** stakeholders.

Delivery (Deliverers)   Deliverers are the people who create change. The **project leader, core team, extended team, invisible team, stakeholders** providing resources, etc.

Emergent Strategy   An emergent strategy is one which is continuously evolving. It is characterised by loosely defined goals and uncertainty about how to proceed. It involves rapid **Plan-Do-Review-Learn cycles**.

Typical emergent strategies often appear to be statements of 'how we got there'. Examples include implementing culture change programmes and realigning business processes with customer demands. In both cases it is easier to define 'what we don't want to be' than 'what we do want to be'.

End User   The end users are the people in the **client organisation** who have to live with the project deliverables. For example they could be the keyboard operators for a new computing system or the shop floor workers and supervisors responsible for quality output once a total quality management initiative has been introduced.

External Projects   Extended team members outside the **core team** who have a distinct role in the delivery of the project.

For external projects most **stakeholders,** and particularly the **client,** are outside the project organisation. With external projects there is often a supplier purchaser relationship. Also see **Commercial projects, Contract** or **Turnkey projects** or **Joint Ventures**.

Fog Project (Fog Walking, Walking in the Fog)   Formally known as an **open** project this type occurs when you are unsure of both what is to be done and how it is to be done.

Going on a Quest   See Quest Projects.

Hard Objectives   These define what the project will deliver. Typically they include the time, cost, specification and terms and conditions.

Illegitimate Projects   Projects which do nothing to help the organisation reach its goals. A project which does not contribute to the current or future profitability of an organisation or any of its other goals. Pet projects and out of date projects where business needs have changed since the project was set up fall into this category.

Invisible Projects   On invisible projects there is little awareness that the project is going on and progress is difficult to see. Writing a new computer programme is an example of a largely invisible project.

Invisible Team   The invisible team comprises all those people within the **project organisation** who are not immediately identified as 'working on the project', yet they have a key input on an occasional basis. For example, the Accounts and Purchasing departments may be important invisible team membes for a project to install new process plant which requires a lot of new equipment and invoices to be paid promptly.

Investment The money an organisation spends on goods/services and information it intends to sell, and all the money it spends on skills, knowledge and equipment to give it the capabilities it needs to generate **throughput**.

Internal Projects For internal projects most **stakeholders**, including the **client**, are inside the project organisation.

Joint Venture Project A hybrid type of project which is both **internally** and/or **externally driven** and **internally** and/or **externally delivered**.

Key Contact The key contact is the focal point of all communications with the **client organisation**. Usually there is a single person in this role who has overall responsibility for the success of the project.

Sometimes the **client organisation** has a team working on the project and there are a number of **key contacts**.

Legitimate Project A project which contributes directly to the goals of an organisation in terms of current or future real revenue or throughput, operating expense or investment.

Managing by Projects A management philosophy which uses projects to achieve strategy. The philosophy extends through all levels and functions of the organisation. Teams are set up to implement particular aspects of the strategy and are dissolved once the desired result is achieved.

At any one time, everyone in the organisation is working on one or more projects. People are recruited to teams on the basis of their relevant knowledge and skills. Everyone working on a project identifies clearly with the project objectives and understands their individual contribution.

Movie Project (Making a Movie) Formally a **semi-open** project. Projects where the means are known but the objective is unclear.

Open Projects (Also see Fog Projects, Movie Projects, Quest Projects) Open projects have loosely defined goals or unclear means. The general direction is understood but the end point is hard to identify. They can be characterised by the statement 'we will get closer than we are'. Examples include implementing total quality programmes, and investing in pure scientific research.

Operating Expense The running cost of the business; all the money that the business spends to produce goods or services it intends to sell – usually equivalent to fixed costs.

Operating Expense Rate The rate at which you need to spend money in order to run a business.

Plan-Do-Review-Learn A plan-do-review-learn cycle involves planning a small step to try something out, completing the step and reviewing progress to see what has been learnt before planning the next step.

Process Consultancy Skills The skills to influence people over whom you have no authority, for example those at higher levels in the organisation. People with a high level of process consultancy skills excel at solving complex issues logically and sorting the solutions for future development. They are also brilliant at reading group dynamics and interpersonal relationships. In addition they are able to make interventions which challenge the basic assumptions underlying decisions.

These skills are critical for the strategic project leader who needs to get inconsistency and ambiguity addressed in order to implement his or her project portfolio, at the same time as retaining respect and support from above.

Project A project is a sequential process which encompasses the definition of project objectives, by reconciling the objectives of a diverse group of stakeholders, then planning, co-ordinating and implementing the activities necessary to achieve these objectives to the satisfaction of the stakeholder group.

Project Objectives These spell out what the project is trying to achieve in terms of hard objectives and soft objectives. They also provide the context for the project in terms of the big picture. In most projects, some new objectives will emerge as the project progresses.

Project Organisation The project organisation is the organisation which employs the project leader and is responsible for carrying out the project.

Project Leadership Project leadership is the discipline of leading and managing projects: leading the visible and invisible teams to achieve the objectives of the stakeholders.

Project Leader The project leader is the person who is accountable for getting the project completed.

Project Portfolio The group of projects which are managed by a strategic project leader. Each project in the portfolio contributes to the achievement of the overall strategy.

Quest Projects (Going on a Quest) Going on a Quest is formally known as a semi-open project. You are clear of what is to be done but clueless about the means.

Real Revenue Rate The rate at which an organisation generates money through sales less real variable costs.

Semi-open Projects See Movie projects.

Semi-closed Projects See Quest projects.

Soft Objectives These relate to how the project should be managed in terms of relationships. Typical soft objectives include how the project should be controlled, how communications are to take place, and what to do in case of emergencies. A project-specific soft objective might be, 'This is very sensitive information, we don't want it widely known.'

Sponsor The person(s) in the project organisation who want(s) the project to be completed. The sponsor is often the project leader's boss but may be a senior manager from a different part of the organisation. Used well, the **sponsor** can provide influence, information, access to an invaluable network and a good sounding board for ideas.

The **Sponsor's** motivation for wanting the project completed is an important part of the big picture. The project leader must understand this motivation in order to manage the relationship successfully.

Some projects do not have a clear sponsor, in which case the project leader needs to return to the big picture, and ask, 'Why do they want it?' and 'Who is the "They" you are referring to?'

In exceptional circumstances, the project leader may also be the sponsor.

Stakeholder   A stakeholder is anyone who has an interest in the project. A typical project has some stakeholders who support it and some who oppose it. A useful way to identify stakeholders is to ask, 'Who is impacted by what this project is trying to achieve?' and then to produce a stakeholder map.

Stakeholder Map   A useful way to understand the relationships between the **stakeholders** is to draw a map. The resulting stakeholder map should show three major groupings of stakeholders, those within the **project organisation**, those within the **client organisation** and those from **supplier** organisations.

Strategic Project Leader   Strategic project leaders act as the conduit between those who formulate strategy and those who implement it on the ground, the project leaders. To be effective in this role they have to understand how strategy is formulated and the problems faced by their project leaders. In addition, they need leadership and process consultancy skills.

Often, a strategic project leader has a project portfolio and acts as the sponsor for each project in the portfolio. Reconciling conflicts between projects and setting priorities are elements of the strategic project leader's job.

Supplier Organisation   Supplier organisations are all those suppliers and sub-contractors, external to the project organisation, who provide the goods and services which are required for the project to be completed.

Throughput   The rate at which an organisation generates money through sales.

See revenue rate.

Turnkey Project   This sort of project is **internally driven** and **externally delivered**. Your organisation pays another organisation to deliver a service.

Visible Projects   On visible projects there is a high level of awareness that the project is going on and progress is easy to see. Building a bridge is an example of a highly visible process.

Visible Team   The visible team are all those within the project organisation who are clearly identified as 'working on the project'. This includes the **core team** and the **extended team**.

Walking in the Fog   See Fog Walking.

OUT OF THE CIRCLE

'Tap, tap, tap.' The door handle tuns slowly and the door swings open.

I lift my head from the manuscript to see who it is. It's Cathy.

'Hello,' she says 'I saw your light on. I thought I would stick my head round your door to see what you were up to working so late.'

You should talk,' I reply. 'What are you doing here?'

'Finishing off a proposal which has to go tomorrow.'

I say, 'That sounds like fun.'

'Not really,' she replies, 'anyway, what are you doing here so late, looking so pleased with yourself?'

I realise that all this time I have had a broad grin on my face. 'I think that I may have solved the problem we had with resourcing the large contract I was worried about earlier.'

'Oh? How?'

'We'll *educate* them, not *consult* to them.'

'What do you mean?' she quizzes.

'We'll help them learn how to manage all change for themselves. That way we can work with more of them, faster, with fewer resources. The real benefit is that they themselves will learn and grow as a result. In the long run it will be easier for them to manage their organisation in these turbulent times, and in the long run it will be cheaper for them.'

Cathy understands what I am saying. 'I see. Educating a business rather than consulting to it. It makes sense. I've often wondered how we will continue to be able to consult effectively if the world gets any faster, so that we don't know the answers ourselves. But you're right, we could educate the business, in order to help it learn itself.' She looks directly at me and says, 'Now I can see why you were grinning.'

'Ah, but that's not the reason I was grinning.' I say.

'What do you mean?' she asks looking confused.

'I was grinning because I will *never have to go round the circle again*!' I exclaim. 'I now understand all change. 1 should be able to get to outcomes I want, rather than have situations conspire against me.'

'What are you talking about with all these conspirators in circles?'

'It's a long story. How about I tell you over a meal?' I suggest.

She greets my idea enthusiastically, 'That's a great idea.'

I say, 'Italian?' It's *deja vu*. Only it isn't. I'm actually remembering a scene from Franck's book. A smile forms on my lips.

'Fine.' she replies.

I finish the scene. 'Do you know any good restaurants around here?'

'Yes there's a great one about five minutes away.'

As she replies, I'm packing up my desk, I pick up the manuscript and shove it into my case. 'OK. I'm ready now. Let's go for it.'

REFERENCES
Sources and further reading

Business

Warren Bennis, *On Becoming A Leader*, Random Century Group Ltd, London. ISBN 0-71269890-6

David Buchanan & David Boddy, *The Expertise of the Change Agent*, Prentice Hall, Hemel Hempsted. ISBN 0-13-544024-6

Wendy Briner, Michael Geddes, Colin Hastings, *Project Leadership*, Gower Publishing Company Ltd, England. ISBN 0-566-02794-1

R. Meredith Belbin, *Management Teams*, William Heinemann Ltd., Oxford. ISBN 0-434-90127-X

Roger Fisher & William Ury, *Getting To Yes*, Random Century Group, London. ISBN 0-09-951730-2

Eliyahu M. Goldratt & Jeff Cox, *The Goal: A process of ongoing improvement*, Gower Publishing, England. ISBN 0-566-02683-X

Eliyahu M. Goldratt & Robert E. Fox, *The Race*, Northern River Press, Croton-on-Hudson, N.Y. ISBN 0-88427-062-9

Charles Handy, *The Age of Unreason*, Arrow Books, London. ISBN 0-09-975740-0

Rosabeth Moss Kanter, *The Change Masters: Corporate Entrepreneurs at Work*, George Allen & Unwin, London. ISBN 0-04-658241-X

Rosabeth Moss Kanter, *When Giants Learn To Dance*, Simon & Schuster, London.

David A. Kolb, *Learning Styles Questionaire: Experimental Learning*, Prentice Hall International Inc., London. ISBN 0-13-295261-0

Eddie Obeng, *Making Re-engineering Happen*, Pitman Publishing, London. 1994

Eddie Obeng, *Solving Unique Problems – Implementing Strategy through Projects*, Pitman Publishing, London. 1994.*

Tom Peters, *Liberation Management: Necessary Disorganisation for the nanosecond Nineties*, Macmillan, London. ISBN 0-333-53340-2

Michael E. Porter, *Competitive Strategy*, Free Press, New York. ISBN 0-02-925360-8

Paul Watzlawick, John H. Weakland & Richard Fisch, *Change*, W.W. Norton & Company, New York. ISBN 0-393-01104-6

Philosophy & Metaphysics

Richard Bach, *Illusions*, William Heinemann Ltd. London. ISBN 0-434-04101-7

Robert M. Prisig, *Zen and the Art of Motorcycle Maintenance*, First Morrow Quill, New York. ISBN 0-688-00230-7

Fiction

Douglas Adams, *Mostly Harmless*, William Heinemann Ltd. London. ISBN 0-434-00926-1

*Strategic Projects Reference.

INDEX

ability, 46–7, 104, 120–1
accomplished change, 46–7, 49–50, 63
accountability, 206
accountants, 16
'action replay', 138–40
activities, 60, 63, 70–2, 82
  breaking down, 59
  constraining, 72
  risk, 190–1
  see also tasks
advantages, 143
aesthetics, 149
agreement/disagreement see conflict
anticipation, 29
attitudes, 102
authority, 18, 82, 190

bad news, 28–9, 195
balance,
  stakeholders, 52–3, 63, 104, 168–75, 195
  teams, 211–14
bar charts, 70, 184
barriers, 52, 101, 150
bartering, 160–1
behaviour, 81, 102, 113, 137, 210–18
  project leaders', 9–10
benchmarking, 44
benefits, making obvious, 143
'big picture', 154, 220
boundaries, defining, 47, 64, 68, 145
breaking down activities, 59
briefings, 5, 26, 39–40, 50–1
'bubbles, blowing', 20, 32–86, 123–37, 145, 151
budgets, 4, 14, 20–1, 107
building site project, 58–9, 61–2
business projects, 16, 18, 37, 52, 77
  complexity, 130–1
  hard and soft criteria, 152, 154
  scheduling resources, 185–6
  specific objectives, 152

cash flows, 69–70, 193
change,
  accomplished, 46–7, 49–50, 63
  changing nature of, 34
  drivers of, 17–18, 104–5, 145, 221
    human constraints and creation, 45–7, 49,
      63–4, 81, 136

human responses to see behaviour
  one leading to another, 43, 49, 63, 83–4, 94,
    186–7
  types, 33–7, 97
  see also 'chunks', change in
change projects, 104, 121, 122, 220
chaos, 43–4, 63, 83–4
checking, 60
choices see options
'chunks', change in, 35, 58, 86, 218
  gaining perspective, 71
  identifying stakeholders, 51–2
  leadership, 80, 81–2, 214–17
circulating information, 27
client organisation, definition of, 220
client sponsor, definition of, 220
clients, 16–17, 39–40, 220
  commercial projects, 105
  identifying stakeholders, 47–8, 50
  internal projects, 104
  problem prediction, 106–11
closed projects, 57–9, 64–5, 99–100, 106
  adaptive approach, 216
  assigning tasks, 79
  balanced teams, 211–13
  definition of, 220
  leadership, 206–7, 211–13, 214, 216
  mechanistic methods, 72
  pacing, 184–5
  risks to completion, 193
co-ordination, 35, 63, 71, 80, 112, 176–83
  breaking down specific activities, 59
  control and risk, 190–3
  poor communication, 11
collaborative projects, 104, 222
commercial projects, 64, 105, 145, 151, 193, 220
commitment, 52–3, 65, 82
communication, 4, 24–5, 27–31, 34, 35–7
  communicating in/out, 140, 194–7
  gaining perspective, 71, 72–3
  plan and task schedules, 188
  updating stakeholders, 11, 48–9, 69–71
competences, 44, 121
competitive advantage, 18, 53, 151–2, 154
  problem prediction, 106–11
completion, 107, 193
computer generated time schedules, 69
computerised management information sytem,

228

Index

Index

Readers with questions or comments may write to me at

Pentacle, The Virtual Business School
Beaconsfield
Buckinghamshire
United Kingdom

Further titles of interest

FINANCIAL TIMES

PITMAN PUBLISHING

ISBN	TITLE	AUTHOR
0 273 60561 5	Achieving Successful Product Change	Innes
0 273 03970 9	Advertising on Trial	Ring
0 273 60232 2	Analysing Your Competitor's Financial Strengths	Howell
0 273 60466 X	Be Your Own Management Consultant	Pinder
0 273 60168 7	Benchmarking for Competitive Advantage	Bendell
0 273 60529 1	Business Forecasting using Financial Models	Hogg
0 273 60456 2	Business Re-engineering in Financial Services	Drew
0 273 60069 9	Company Penalties	Howarth
0 273 60558 5	Complete Quality Manual	McGoldrick
0 273 03859 1	Control Your Overheads	Booth
0 273 60022 2	Creating Product Value	De Meyer
0 273 60300 0	Creating World Class Suppliers	Hines
0 273 60383 3	Delayering Organisations	Keuning
0 273 60171 7	Does Your Company Need Multimedia?	Chatterton
0 273 60003 6	Financial Engineering	Galitz
0 273 60065 6	Financial Management for Service Companies	Ward
0 273 60205 5	Financial Times Guide to Using the Financial Pages	Vaitilingam
0 273 60006 0	Financial Times on Management	Lorenz
0 273 03955 5	Green Business Opportunities	Koechlin
0 273 60385 X	Implementing the Learning Organisation	Thurbin
0 273 03848 6	Implementing Total Quality Management	Munro-Faure
0 273 60025 7	Innovative Management	Phillips
0 273 60327 2	Investor's Guide to Emerging Markets	Mobius
0 273 60622 0	Investor's Guide to Measuring Share Performance	Macfie
0 273 60528 3	Investor's Guide to Selecting Shares that Perform	Koch
0 273 60704 9	Investor's Guide to Traded Options	Ford
0 273 03751 X	Investor's Guide to Warrants	McHattie
0 273 03957 1	Key Management Ratios	Walsh
0 273 60384 1	Key Management Tools	Lambert
0 273 60259 4	Making Change Happen	Wilson
0 273 60424 4	Making Re-engineering Happen	Obeng
0 273 60533 X	Managing Talent	Sadler
0 273 60153 9	Perfectly Legal Competitor Intelligence	Bernhardt
0 273 60167 9	Profit from Strategic Marketing	Wolfe
0 273 60170 9	Proposals, Pitches and Beauty Parades	de Forte
0 273 60616 6	Quality Tool Kit	Mirams
0 273 60336 1	Realising Investment Value	Bygrave
0 273 60713 8	Rethinking the Company	Clarke
0 273 60328 0	Spider Principle	Linton
0 273 03873 7	Strategic Customer Alliances	Burnett
0 273 03949 0	Strategy Quest	Hill
0 273 60624 7	Top Intrapreneurs	Lombriser
0 273 03447 2	Total Customer Satisfaction	Horovitz
0 273 60201 2	Wake Up and Shake Up Your Company	Koch
0 273 60387 6	What Do High Performance Managers Really Do?	Hodgson

For further details or a full list of titles contact:

The Professional Marketing Department, Pitman Publishing, 128 Long Acre, London WC2E 9AN, UK
Tel +44 (0)71 379 7383 or fax +44 (0)71 240 5771